Jesus Ascended. What Does That Mean?

JESUS' FINAL 40-DAY LESSON

SCOTT DOUGLAS

SD Publications
Anaheim, California

For Miko Rey La Counte

Table of Contents

INTRODUCTION

....

SOMETHING HAPPENED

Something happened.

Jesus rose. We hear about it every Easter. We sing songs about it. We even have an Easter Bunny to symbolize the event.[1]

But Christ didn't just rise from the dead. He ascended to Heaven.

We hear the stories about Peter and John and all the heroes of the New Testament, and they're unstoppable Christians—fearless and bold. And sometimes we wrongly assume that they just got that way. That Christ died for their sins, and bam! They're instantly changed! On the contrary, the disciples were actually quite cowardly in their actions after the Resurrection.

---

[1] Fun fact about Easter Bunnies—people used to believe that they were hermaphrodites (i.e., they could reproduce without having sex). You know who else could do that? The Virgin Mary! Hence, the Easter Bunny was born.

It wasn't until after the Ascension that they were on fire for Christ. So, what happened during the forty days? Something happened.

You'd think that everyone and their brother would want to talk about an event that incredible. But you'd be wrong. And it leaves us with more than a few questions.

Where do you go if you want to understand what happened? Matthew? You won't find it there. Mark? Kind of, but it's text that most Bible scholars now accept was not in the earliest version. What about John? Surely good old John would have a lot to say! Not exactly. He talks about Jesus doing miracles, but nowhere in John does he ascend to Heaven.

So how is it that Christians came to believe that Jesus not only rose from the dead, but stuck around forty days before ascending to Heaven? That's where Luke comes in. Luke is the only Gospel that talks at any length (even though it's short passages) about Jesus ascending. He does so in both the Gospel of Luke and the Acts of the Apostles, which he also authored.

Sprinkled throughout the Bible are references to the Ascension, which tells us that it was something early Christians believed. The Apostle Peter believed it,[2] as did the Apostle

---

[2] 1 Peter 3:13-22

Paul,[3] and it's fair to say that all the other apostles did as well.[4]

So important is the doctrine, that the original statement of belief that most Christians (Catholic, Protestant, and Orthodox) go to—the Nicene Creed—includes it. That means if you belong to any of those groups, you are kind of supposed to believe in the Ascension.[5]

#   #   #

A Not Completely Necessary Detour of Empty Tomb Theories

The point of this book isn't to prove that the Resurrection is real; there are plenty of books on that. Still, as a reference only, I will note the popular theories about what else could have happened.

The LCD Theory

This theory says what is depicted in the Bible is really just a series of hallucinations. That makes sense. It might even be logical. But there are two problems:

---

[3] Ephesians 4:8-10

[4] See Appendix A for a more complete list of Ascension references.

[5] Even if you don't have the slightest idea about what it is or means.

First, more than one person saw him—even 500 at one time. If Peter saw him but no one else did, it would be easy to dismiss it as a hallucination. But all the disciples (minus Judas) saw him, the women saw him, and strangers saw him.

Also, I've had some pretty weird dreams;[6] but here's the thing about my dreams—and the dreams of most people—they don't convict you to die for your dream. Hundreds of Christians had no problem dying for what they saw, and a vision just doesn't give you that kind of conviction.

The Thieving Disciples

One of the more popular beliefs amongst people who believe the tomb was empty, but that Jesus did not rise from the dead, is that his body was stolen—most likely by the disciples who were disappointed that Jesus did not rise on his own.

This theory makes pretty good sense. Your leader dies; you're in denial; and you don't want to believe you just spent years of your life with a false teacher…so you steal his body to make people believe it's true.

---

[6] The one where my dog was my mother, and he (yes, for an even weirder reason my dog mother was a he) told me to become a doctor of medicine specializing in soda…that was a weird dream.

There are a number of problems with this theory. They were in a pretty hopeless place and didn't know what to make of the events that transpired. There is absolutely no reason to steal his body because they would gain nothing in doing so. Nobody would gain anything by stealing the body—not the disciples, not the Romans, not the women, and not the Jewish people. The gospel records Jesus' linens being in the tomb; why steal a body without the linens? "Hey guys, let's steal Jesus' body, but for good measure let's make him naked because everyone knows dead people like to feel the breeze."

The Swoon Theory

This theory says that Jesus didn't really die; he just fainted and was put in the tomb alive; after several hours, he woke up and left the tomb. The disciples only mistook him as being dead.

The problems with this theory are plentiful. First, the Gospel of John[7] says that the linen used to wrap him was still there—meaning that Jesus would have had to wiggle out of the wraps. And once he wiggled out, he—a man who had just spent the past several hours being beaten, hung on a cross, pierced at the side—would have had to move the stone away and

---

[7] John 20:5

further fight off the guard who was guarding the tomb.

So, what's the deal with the Ascension anyway? Shouldn't this be plastered all over the place? Wouldn't there have been a giant atomic bomb-sized glorious viewing that you could see all the way from Rome? Why did only believers see it?

First, it is referenced outside the Bible—more on that in later chapters.

Second, we have to consider the nature of Christ. He performed miracles, but that was never his ministry. He didn't come to Earth to be the flashy miracle guy. His ministry was the way he lived his life.

People frequently say, "If there is a God, then why doesn't he announce it?" What I often think about this phrase is "Doesn't he?" Every day, things happen that are beyond science—things that can only be described by the word miraculous. They deeply move us—heck sometimes we even like them on Facebook. But the thing is, miracles are forgotten pretty quickly. You are quicker to forget a miracle than you are a simple kind gesture in a time of need.

And let's not forget, if God did announce himself, the whole freewill thing would go out the window. If we could walk outside right now, look up and see God up in the sky, then why wouldn't we believe in him? But unfortunately, on Earth we can't have that kind of relationship.

So, in answer to that question about why people didn't see it from miles away, the reason is probably as simple as it was not all that spectacular. Jesus didn't ride up to Heaven on an atomic bomb with a cowboy hat, shooting out fireworks from his eyeballs. It was more likely a beautifully intimate moment witnessed by those closest to him. It wasn't meant for the entire Roman Empire to see.

#   #   #

So, we have this intimate event that only a select few even saw. Great. But why is that event even important?

Close your eyes and take a road trip through history with me; we're about to get Biblical, so buckle in.[8]

Think back to those early Sunday school stories; the ones about the fall of Eden, Noah, the Tower of Babel, Moses. They're great stories and even better lessons for history...but they also have a theme. The entire Old Testament has a theme, in fact. God's people mess up and they fall; God picks them up and they excel; God's people mess up and they fall; God picks them up and they excel. It's like a bad broken record. If you've ever read the Old Testament from cover to cover, you probably asked yourself at least fifty times, "Seriously, what's wrong with these people? Why can't they just listen to God?!"

The Jewish people were privileged in the sense that they knew no matter how badly they screwed up, God would eventually rescue them, and all would be well again. They expected it. The prophets predicting a Messiah who would rule over them should really not be all that surprising—of course God would send someone to rescue them. They had

---

[8] Don't worry, we'll stick to Sunday school stories.

messed up, and the kingdom God had given them with David had been taken away, so of course a new king from David's line would come and rescue them. That's just the way God did things—God's redemption was just as predictable as Israel's sin.

The Ascension is the fulfillment of this promise. When Jesus left Earth, he created a new kingdom in the line of David in Heaven. This pattern of God's people sinning, and God's people being redeemed could finally be resolved once and for all.

Lots of men and women have been raised from the dead; the Resurrection of Christ is really nothing special. Sure, it's an amazing, unexplained feat that can only be attributed to divine intervention, but pause for a moment and ask: what's so special about the Resurrection? Christ raised dead people; so did his disciples. Yeah, it's pretty amazing that he rose from the dead, but if that in itself is enough to worship a person, shouldn't we also be praying to people like Lazarus?[9]

The amazing thing about the Resurrection is not the act, but the act that followed—the theology that feels more like a footnote in history: The Ascension. Which leaves us with a very important question to ask: If it's so important, then why is it only mentioned in the Gospel of Luke? Why isn't the Ascension mentioned more often in the Gospels?

------

[9] Lazarus, for those who need a reminder, came back to life after being dead for four days after Jesus came and woke him up.

Jesus Ascended. What Does That Mean?

First, let's consider dates. More than likely, Luke and John were the last Gospels written, which means they had more time to digest things. The Resurrection, by human standards, is more fascinating to tell, and there's a chance that the early writers of the Gospel hadn't quite considered the significance of what happened.

Let's also considered the missing fragment of Mark; it cuts off in a very unusual place. Most scholars agree that the ending in place was not by the original author...but most scholars also believe where it cuts off isn't the original ending. So, what are we left with? The most popular theory is that while the added text isn't completely Mark, it isn't completely not Mark either. What does that mean? It means there's a very strong chance that the original version of Mark did mention the Ascension—just not quite like the translator wrote it—perhaps with different syntax, but the same meaning.

The most important thing to remember about the Gospels is they were written with an audience in mind. Think about Abraham Lincoln; there have been over 15,000 books written about him. How can people still make money writing about Lincoln? Easy...they write about him from different angles that people haven't considered. Some biographers will spend little or no time writing about Lincoln's death because that's not what their book is about. So, when we think about why the Gospels each wrote different accounts of the post-Resurrection, it's because each one was writing for a different purpose.

#   #   #

The Audience of the Gospels

There's a lot to digest, so let's take a short break. As we consider why the Ascension isn't clearly recorded in all the Gospels, let's consider the purpose of each Gospel (i.e. who they were writing to and what their intent was).

Matthew

Audience: Early tradition said the Gospel of Matthew was written by Matthew, the disciple; more recent scholars tend to believe that because Matthew seems to use Mark as a source, it may have been someone else.[10] Whatever the case, the Gospel of Matthew seems to have been written with Jews in mind; Matthew wanted to prove that Christ was the Messiah that the Jewish people had been waiting for.

Resurrection Message: The Gospel of Matthew ends with the Great Commission, in which Jesus instructs the disciples to go and make disciples of all nations. It's fitting that Matthew ended with Jesus telling the disciples to go and convert, because that's what his Gospel was all about—to tell the good news and teach

---

[10] Such as a follower of Matthew.

about the new covenant.

Mark

Audience: Like Matthew, it's difficult to say who the author of Mark's Gospel is, but it's traditionally held that the author is John Mark—who was close to the Apostle Peter and likely based his Gospel on Peter's teaching. Mark's reference to Jewish customs that Jewish believers would already know suggests that Mark intended his book for Gentiles who weren't familiar with Jewish customs.

Resurrection Message: Mark's Resurrection message is the trickiest; not because it's hard to understand, but because it's hard to know what he actually wrote. The earliest versions of Mark stop midsentence with the trembling women who have found the empty tomb. Most scholars accept that there is truth to Mark 16:9-20, but there is debate about what was and wasn't in the actual Gospel. If you believe that the Gospel ended at verse 9, then the message clearly says that Christ rose, but there was probably confusion about what this meant.

Luke

Audience: Traditionally, the author of the Gospel of Luke was a physician and companion to the Apostle Paul named Luke. Luke was concerned with preserving an accurate historic record of what really happened. By the time the Gospel was written, there were a growing number of false teachings, and it seems that Luke set out to write out the real story for believers.

Resurrection Message: Luke paints a very vivid picture of both the Resurrection and Ascension; he obviously wanted the most non-biased, historically accurate report possible, so he also wanted to also give the most complete story.

John

Audience: The author's reference to himself seems to correctly imply that the Gospel of John was written by the Apostle John. John, by this point, had already seen the persecution of many of his Christian brothers and sisters, and it seems likely that he is writing the Gospel to build up those who believe while also earning new converts. John's style of philosophical writing is also appealing to Greek thinkers, so, while it may not have been his intent, it is easy to see that audience would have found the message appealing.

Resurrection Message: Like Luke, John also gives a detailed account of post-Resurrection events. John states the most important things but concludes on a hopeful note by noting that Jesus did many other things and there's absolutely no way any book could contain all of it.

While not all the Gospels end with the Ascension, there are plenty of references to it;[11] further the Ascension is referenced later in the letters and epistles. The intent of the Gospels was to tell the good news of the life and Resurrection of Christ; to the early church, the Ascension represented a sad time—a separation of the person they had devotedly followed. While writing a Gospel with the intention of converting a non-believer, the Ascension is not the most fitting in the story.

The Resurrection was great. I believe in it. I believe it was miraculous. But I don't believe that Christ is Lord because he rose from the dead.

There's more written about Christ's ministry before his death than the events that happened after his Resurrection, but when we look at Ascension, we begin to see that there's power in small details. We begin to see that something happened after the Resurrection—something happened to trans-

---

[11] See the Appendix for a more comprehensive list.

form the lives of believers and make them more than followers.

The problem with the Resurrection of Christ is as believers we have a tendency to believe in the miracle and not the theology. When we look at what happened after the Resurrection, and further at the Ascension of Christ, we begin to see what happened to transform the followers—and in seeing this we might just be transformed ourselves.

Something did indeed happen during the forty days; why didn't God spend more time revealing? That's something that we will not know on Earth. But when we look at what he does reveal in the Ascension, we begin to see that Jesus was not done teaching; and as we begin to understand these teachings, we will be transformed ourselves.

UNSTOPPABLE CHRISTIANS

The apostles and first Christians weren't the only ones who were unstoppable; over the past 2000 some odd years, lots of Christians have done amazing and even miraculous things. In each chapter, I'll look at one unstoppable Christian you've probably never heard of.

It makes sense that the first person should literally be unstoppable. That brings us to...Denis.

Denis was the Bishop of the City of Love: Paris. He lived in the third century AD. Unfortunately for the

Bishop, the City of Love wasn't so loving in the third century.

In 250 AD, the Emperor Decius issued an edict that said everyone must perform a sacrifice to the Roman gods. The edict is of note because it is the first time that legislation had forced Christians to decide between the church and state—or belief and death. The intended target was obviously Christians because Jews were exempt from such laws by having the status of religio licita (or permitted religion).

While there's nothing to support just how enforced the edict was, several very prominent Christians were martyred as a result. Because Denis was a well-known member of the church, it wasn't long before Rome came knocking.

Denis refused to perform the sacrifice, and he was ordered to be executed by beheading.

Here's where things get interesting—albeit divine—Denis' head is cut off...but he doesn't die! He picks up his head, continues preaching, and walks six miles before finally falling to his death.

A church was built to honor him: The Cathedral Basilica of Saint Denis in Saint-Denis, France.

ONE

....

JESUS APPEARS TO THE MARYS

M ore people believe in angels than in hell. And why not? It's far easier to believe in good things than bad. Unfortunately, most people believe in the Nicolas Cage kind of angels;[12] the kind of angel that humans can actually become if they're swell people; the kind that have wings and float around just waiting to save us. That's not necessarily false, but it's not exactly Biblical.[13]

So, when the gospels record angels at the empty tomb of Christ, it's important to remember what angels are in the Bible—to put it simply, angels are messengers from God.

There's an important lesson to be learned about the women Jesus is about to appear to, but before we get to that, we have to understand the angels.

---

[12] Fun fact—City of Angels steals several plot points from Hans Christian Andersen's *The Little Mermaid.*

[13] Meg Ryan isn't even a Bible name.

Jesus Ascended. What Does That Mean?

Depending on the gospel account, there was between one to four angels at the tomb; contradictory, right? Not exactly. Remember, the Gospels are four different writers with four different purposes writing for four different audiences. They aren't contradicting each other; they're recording different aspects of the same story.

The greater importance isn't on the detail—how many angels there were—it's on the meaning of the details. What, if anything, do the angels mean? If angels are Heavenly messengers, then what is it that they are announcing?

First, it's obvious that their message is that Jesus has resurrected, and he is the Messiah. Just as gospels noted that angels were there to announce his birth, they are there to announce his resurrection.

But there's more. The Gospel of John gives an important detail in 20:11. He says that two angels were sitting.

Impressive, right? It's not every day you read about two angels sitting on the job. More curious, however, is not what they're doing, but where they're doing it—they're sitting where Jesus' body was only a short time ago.

It's time to get all Old Testament. The Old Testament is notorious for laws—lots and lots of laws.[14] Some laws that make sense[15] and some are a little...odd.[16] But tucked in there with all of those laws is a lot of stuff about a certain

---

[14] 613 laws to be exact.

[15] There's one God; worship him.

[16] They made sense thousands of years ago, but they really have no importance today.

Ark of the Covenant. The Ark was built in Moses' time and they took that bad boy everywhere. It represented God's covenant with the Israelites and it's a permanent fixture throughout the Old Testament.

So, what does that have to do with two angels sitting where Jesus was? On top of the Ark were statues of two cherubim—or angels.

What the Gospel of John is painting is a real-life Ark of the Covenant. They aren't just sitting back on the tomb's recliners—they're sitting on the stone that held Jesus' body; John's record is saying, "Guess what? There's a new covenant in town."

#   #   #

When Apple rolls out a new iPhone, what do they do? They hold a big press conference that's meant to get their base followers excited and then they'll go out and tell their friends who will also get excited, and before you know it millions of people have new phones. Every company uses the same strategy—market to your base—your product evangelist.

It makes sense that God would market his new covenant the same way—he'd tell his disciples all about it, so they could go spread the news to the world. But something unusual happens on the way to the podium to make the big announcement—God markets it to the audience you'd least likely suspect: the women.

It would be like Apple going to a third world where there's absolute zero cellular signal, Wi-Fi, or electricity and saying, "Isn't this cool?" I'm sure they'd think it was pretty amazing, but what are they supposed to do with it?

Today a woman is just as likely to start a revolution as a man; two thousand years ago? Not so much. So, what is God thinking? What's he trying to teach us here?

If you are a Bible conspiracy theorist, then it isn't at all surprising—Jesus was, after all, doing the old bait n' tackle with her; hints and blatant descriptions of Jesus and Mary locking lips are in all the ancient manuscripts. Unfortunately for Biblical conspiracy theorists, the ancient manuscripts come to light too long after Jesus' life to make them anything but just stories people were telling. The simple fact is there's nothing in the Gospels to suggest that Jesus was involved in a relationship with Mary.[17]

So, if it's not because he wanted to see his old sweetheart, then why? Was it because he was a card-carrying member of the local feminist movement of Jerusalem, and he wanted to set his boys straight on who he *really* loves? Not likely.[18]

So, what gives? There are 11 confused men who risk an awful lot to follow Jesus. Couldn't Jesus have done them a solid and let them know all was well? Of course! But he didn't...and that certainly begs the question why.

---

[17] In the words of Seinfeld, "Not that there's anything wrong with that"—it just didn't happen.

[18] Jesus was pretty radical in thinking with regard to women, but his appearance here doesn't seem to imply it has anything to do with making a feminist statement.

On the surface, the best reason is simply because the Marys were the least likely suspects for a crime. If one of the disciples had gotten to the tomb first, then people could have more easily said they stole his body—heck, they didn't even go to the tomb first and people still say this!

The fact that it was a woman who was the first eyewitness makes it more believable for the mere fact that women would not be able to carry out the plot to steal his body—they'd have to roll away a large stone, carry a rather heavy body, and fight off Roman guards. There are plenty of women who could carry off this plot—they're called women warriors and they're champions in swordplay; Brienne of Tarth from *Game of Thrones*—she might be able to pull it off…but these women? Not so much.

But God rarely teaches us things on the surface. There's something much deeper and personal about what's about to happen. The disciples had a much different relationship with Jesus than the women did.

The first lesson Jesus gives post-Resurrection is about the relationship we can have with him.

#   #   #

Before getting too far along, let's address the elephant in the room. The women appear first in all four of the Gospels…kind of. When you read all the accounts side by side,[19] each gospel tells a slightly different story. Some mention that Jesus appeared in front of several women, others say it was only Mary Magdalene. Some say Mary went to the

---

[19] For added challenge, you can also read them all upside-down.

tomb, saw it was empty, told the others, then went back to the tomb.

So, are we really to believe that the Gospel is to be trusted when we have four different books saying four contradictory things? If they got this all messed up, they must have gotten the rest all messed up. That's certainly a fair point, but to call the accounts contradictory is a bit extreme—and wrong.

In reality, it can be assumed it was several women, but because Mary Magdalene was kind of like the Peter of women, that's who they mentioned.[20] As noted in the previous chapter, each author had a different audience; some of those audiences would have not known who all the Marys or other women were, but they definitely knew who Mary Magdalene was. It would be like a newspaper saying Pope Francis and Federico Lombardi flew to Germany to visit a church; Federico Lombardi is an important person in the Catholic Church, but most people don't know who he is—so what you are more likely to read is that Pope Francis flew to Germany to visit a church.

The different accounts are not an example of contradiction; rather, they are an example of different authors.

#   #   #

There's Something About Marys

---

[20] She's kind of a rock star.

Who were these women that all the Gospels mention? Let's pause for a section and get a pop-up mini biography.

MARY MAGDALENE

Luke 8:2 and Mark 16:9 say that she was a woman Jesus had cured and cast out seven demons from. Most see her as the person that women turned to as a leader in the early church—in the same way men might have looked at Peter. Some have called her a repentant prostitute, but this largely stems from the misunderstanding that she was the unnamed sinner who anoints Jesus' feet; most scholars agree that she was not. This misconception was helped along by Pope Gregory, who delivered a sermon that misattributed Mary with the unnamed sinner. Pope Gregory based this on the fact that the seven demons were really seven sins and those seven sins obviously represented her loose lifestyle. Speculation that she was in a relationship with Jesus was first seen in the Gospel of Philip;[21] in it, Jesus is seen kissing Mary in a way that offended the disciples who wanted to know why he loved her more than them.

---

[21] Apocryphal text written most likely in the third century—so the first conspiracy theory about Jesus' love-life isn't documented for 300 years.

SALOME

Salome is only briefly mentioned in the Bible, but the fact that she is mentioned at all shows that she is important. So, who was she? Depends on who you ask; Catholic tradition holds that she is one of the Three Marys. The most popular tradition, however, is that she's the mother of James and John—she is also sometimes referred to as the sister of Mary...or Jesus' aunt. If you dig deeper into early Christian apocryphal text,[22] you find Salome mentioned quite a bit more; an infancy gospel called Protevangelion of James cites Salome as a midwife at the birth of Jesus. She is also often confused with Herod's daughter, also named Salome, whose erotic dance during Herod's birthday bash gave her mom the opportunity to ask for John the Baptist's head on a plate.

MARY, MOTHER OF JAMES

Mary is basically known for witnessing Jesus' death on the cross at a distance and seeing the empty tomb. Even apocryphal text seems to be mum on who she might have been. So, all we know is that she was the mother of James the Less.

---

[22] Meaning that their truth cannot be verified.

JOANNA

Finally, it's worth noting that the women present for this event may not have been all Marys. Some speculate that one of the women was Joanna—a woman mentioned earlier in Luke. (Luke 8:2-3) Not a lot is known about Joanna except that she was married to Chuza, who managed Herod Antipas' household.

The angels just performed the opening act of the most epic rock concert ever—now it's time for the main act to perform his final set list of teachings before ascending to Heaven—and spoiler alert, his set list includes all of his greatest hits. In John 20:16, Jesus starts with a bang when he says something incredibly telling. He says, "Mary."

At first glance, it doesn't seem like much, but let's look at what's going on.

Mary is an emotional wreck. Her savior is gone. She can't make sense of what's happened. She's a mess!

Jesus appears to her and she's so emotional that she doesn't even know who she's talking to. She's in complete denial.

It's in this denial that it gets interesting.

Mary just devoted years of her life devoted to following this guy and now he's alive and in the flesh standing right in front of her...and she has no clue that it's him! That's a little odd, isn't it? When odd things happen in the Bible, we should never just shrug and say, "That was weird" and move on. We should look at it curiously and say is there something more going on here?

There's definitely more going on here. The scene is a mirror image of us.

When we don't believe, we're in denial. Jesus is standing right in front of us, but we just think we're talking to a stranger and we don't recognize him. We can't see Jesus until we are ready to accept Jesus. And in that moment, Mary just isn't ready because she still can't comprehend any of it.

But with one word, Mary snaps out of it. She can see Jesus and it all makes sense. She knows who he is.

Jesus doesn't do what some of us might. If I'd just risen from the dead and appeared in front of my wife and she didn't know me, I wouldn't say, "Diana." I'd shake her and say, "Are you kidding me! All these years together and you don't know who I am? What the heck is wrong with you?" And then I'd storm off and pout.

But Jesus says, "Mary." And with that word she knows Jesus is alive and standing in front of her.

Jesus could have said any word, but he chose her name. To snap her out of her denial, he told her he knew her name—he knew who she was. It's an intimate gesture and what it shows is that Jesus knows each of us personally. He knows our name.

But here's the funny thing about what happens next. Mary and Jesus just had a moment. It's intimate. It's personal. It's time to hug it up. But that doesn't happen.

The touchy-feely Jesus that's all over the New Testament is suddenly a little less...touchy.

There are a lot of polar opposites in the post-Resurrection—things you'd expect to be happening aren't happening.

Mary goes for the hug and Jesus hug blocks her. John 20:17 says that Jesus told her not to touch him because he had not ascended to Heaven.

So, let's get this straight. Jesus—the guy Christians grow up believing we can have a personal relationship with is telling her she can't hug him? That doesn't seem too personal.

At face value, it's not personal at all. Later, Thomas gets to touch Jesus, so why him and not Mary?

The fact that Thomas could touch him but not Mary tells us that when Jesus says not to touch him, it's not because he can't be touched.

Mary wants to embrace him because she thinks it's back to the good old days—chilling in the countryside listening to amazing sermons, feeding thousands, and getting tipsy on the best water-to-wine ever made. But Jesus is telling her that the good old days are gone—she needs to know him differently now. The good old days are really in front of her, but she needs to come to understand what that means.

From that point on, he needed Mary to know that the relationship would be a spiritual one—not a physical one.

There are two Jesuses. Some of us only get to know one. There's the one we all come to know—the one who did amazing things. One might call him the historical Jesus. And then there's one we know if we commit our life to him; this is the spiritual Jesus.

Jesus' refusal to Mary isn't because she can't touch him; it's because she can't touch him like before.

Everyone wants to see Jesus. If they could just have a bit of proof, they'd believe. But that Jesus isn't here anymore. The Jesus we can know is the one we know spiritually.

But the one we know spiritually we can know much more intimately than the one who came in the flesh. Before the Resurrection, Jesus was the great teacher; what's happening is the start of the transformation for believers—they are about to go from students to teachers.

And finally, we come to what may be the most jarring verse of all to some readers—especially modern readers who are not reading the original translation and may miss the context. Jesus gives specific instructions to Mary; he says to tell them, "I am ascending to my Father and your Father, to my God and your God." (NIV) [23]

Huh?

First, let's consider something very important here. Jesus could have just as easily said "our Father" and "our God." He didn't.

Let's hit the rewind button here a second and visit just a few chapters prior: John 5:16-18.

This is one of the first things that gets Jesus in a whirlwind of trouble with Jewish leaders. First, he heals on the

---

[23] John 20:17

Sabbath—a major no-no.[24] Jesus was a good talker; he probably could have gotten away with it by talking his way out, but he has no intention of running away. Instead he uses the phrase "My Father." That does it! The Jewish leaders are fuming because this phrase puts Jesus as an equal to God.

What Jesus is telling Mary is that he is equal to God...but he doesn't stop there. He is saying that the man upstairs is now "your Father" and "your God." Father is a reference to the divine nature of Christ, and God is a reference to his human nature (i.e., God in the Flesh). Christ has now secured our place and through him we can have unity with God.

Some of the Gospels simply reported that Mary and the others saw Jesus and he told them to go tell the disciples; that's essentially what John says. But John found it to be important to his message to relate what Jesus said to Mary.

John was traditionally the last Gospel written; perhaps in his old age, he had come to realize the importance women had played in Jesus' ministry and he wanted to portray them fairly. But more importantly, John wants his readers to know that they can have unity with God—that God doesn't have to be the mighty killjoy in the sky—that through Christ, we can have a relationship with God that's like belonging to a family.

There's going to be many lessons to transform the disciples lives post-Resurrection, but the first is about the relationship they now have with God.

---

[24] Sabbaths are for obeying God, not experiencing God.

Jesus Ascended. What Does That Mean?

Everyone knows the phrase, "You can have a personal relationship with God." But the nature of people can make that phrase carry less meaning, because Christians sometimes look at other Christians and expect them to have the same personal relationship that they have.

Having a personal relationship isn't about the other person. It's about you. Jesus Christ knows your name. He knows your struggles. Your pains. He knows your background. He knows what makes you angry; what makes you sad; what makes you want to give up—and what makes you want to keep going. He knows everything about you.

We all have struggles. Some of us it is addictions. Some of us it is pride. Some it is greed. Whatever it is: Jesus knows our name. He knows all of our weaknesses and he's returned to dwell inside us—to experience an intimacy with him that we would not know without the Resurrection.

But first we have to be like Mary: we have to see him. We can say we know Jesus just like Mary said she knew him. But knowing Jesus and seeing Jesus are two different things. We can go to church and know about Jesus—about his teachings, about what he did, and his theology; we can do all of that without ever really seeing Jesus—without ever really knowing what it means to have a true relationship with Jesus.

To see Jesus is to put all your pains aside and accept that Jesus really does want to dwell in you—he really does love you and he really is there with you. He really does know your name.

UNSTOPPABLE CHRISTIANS

Catherine of Siena is one of the top religious women of all time—right up there with Mary, Mary, and Other Mary. When most women of her day (she lived from 1347-1380) were content being submissive, she was quite the bad girl by actually using her mind and writing some of the greatest works of early Christian literature. Unfortunately, Catherine was also kind of anorexic for Jesus. Communion became one of her few meals in later life (and by later, we're talking late 20s).

Her fasting was legendary and ultimately fatal; by the age of 33, she could no longer eat or swallow water, and she died of a stroke. People of her day loved her—so much so that they wanted her body in Siena. But there was a problem—you couldn't just drag a smelly corpse out of Rome. Mourners decided that if they couldn't have the body, they could at least have the head. They chopped it off, stuffed it in a bag, and left for Siena; according to legends, when guards questioned what the foul-smelling bag was, they opened it up and there were roses inside. Fans of the morbid can see the head for themselves by visiting the Basilica di San Domenico.

TWO

....

CLEOPAS AND SOME OTHER GUY

W e've heard the stories. Maybe we've even been the story. Something tragic happens—let's just say a bad accident. And in our moment of distress, a person is with us who comforts us and even helps us. Then they leave and we ask someone, "Hey, where's that person who was helping me?" And they say, "What person? You've been alone the whole time." In the words of the great philosopher Keanu Reeves: "Whoa!" What happens next could easily bring out the "Whoa!" in Keanu.

Jesus has just performed his opening act for the women—we can know Jesus personally, and it's now time for some time with his boys, the disciples. But about that...

Continuing on with the pattern of things not happening that you would expect to happen, Jesus doesn't visit his disciples. Instead, he appears to two somewhat random characters—one whose name is given (Cleopas), but who we still know pretty much nothing about, and one who's so irrelevant to the story, the name is not even mentioned.

With Mary, Jesus showed us how he knew us, but with these men, he's going to show us the place we need to be in to be able to see him. Anyone can "say" they have a personal relationship with Jesus Christ, but Jesus is going to show us with these men how we can prepare ourselves for an authentic relationship—one where we don't just know Christ, but experience him.

Luke 24:34 does mention there was a meeting with Peter before he met these two men; I'll come back to that in the next chapter. But Luke finds it important to mention this story before he references Peter, and he has good reason: the message here is important to both the spread of Christianity and our growth as Christians. Peter's meeting is personal; this meeting is transparent.

As with many things in the Bible, God doesn't reveal why he appears to these two random characters first. One can speculate that it's perhaps because the focus is on the teaching and not who is being taught—the disciples aren't the heroes of the Gospel, the message is. By not appearing to them it helps deemphasize their role in that message.

So, if the message and not the people is important, then what is the message being conveyed here?

Let's look first at where they are going: Emmaus.

If you want to go to a map, you can locate Emmaus right smack in the middle of somewhere. That's because no one actually knows where Emmaus is—or rather was. The city did exist; several sources cite various places with that name. The trouble is there are only theories about where it is.

So, is it so important that no one even knows where on Earth it is? That doesn't sound too important. And that's half right. It could have been Emmaus, or it could have been any other place. Luke doesn't tell us the name so we can all hightail it to the Middle East for a pilgrimage—he tells us the name so we know this is a true account. This event happened. He wants to make sure the reader knows this isn't a mythological story that is only symbolically or metaphorically true. If he had merely said, "Jesus met these two guys on the road," then one could interpret it as just a story. But he doesn't do that. These two guys had a destination.

Next, let's look at how Jesus appeared to them. Jesus appears several different ways post-Resurrection. In this appearance, it seems that Jesus doesn't just appear, but rather walks up behind them. Had he just appeared, then the story might have taken a different toll, because it would be much easier for these two men to see a miracle has appeared right in front of their eyes. Jesus doesn't want these men to witness a miracle—he wants them to have a connection.

It's the same connection we have. Jesus is God—do you really think that if he wanted to, he couldn't appear to you right as you read this passage and say, "What's up?!" He could! But he probably didn't. He doesn't want you to believe because of a miracle; he wants to really understand what the Resurrection is.

Cleopas and his companion take a lot of heat for not knowing who Jesus is; while these men aren't part of the core twelve, it's implied that they should have known better—they should have been able to recognize Jesus. But they don't. It's not all on them, however; the Bible says they were "kept" from recognizing him.[25] Why would they be "kept" from recognizing him? Let's mark that as "to be continued" and come back to it later.

Will the Real Cleopas Please Stand Up?

There are many traditions about who Cleopas was (and wasn't) over the years, three theories in particular have become popular:

Cleopas Was Cleophas — Hegesippus, an early chronicler of the church, wrote in 180 A.D. that he had interviewed a grandson of Jude the Apostle; the grandson claimed that Cleopas was Cleophas, who was the brother of Joseph (husband of the Virgin Mary).

Cleopas Was Clopas — John 19:25 references Clopas, who is traditionally viewed as either the husband of Mary Magdalene or the father of Mary Magdalene. She is recorded as "Mary of Clopas" which means, depending on who you ask, "Mary, wife of Clopas" or "Mary, daughter of Clopas."

---

[25] Luke 24:16

Cleopas Was Cleopas — The figure so prominent in the story may have simply been an important figure in the early church who was never recorded anywhere else and thus his importance has been lost over the years.

Translations are a messy business and, with names especially, it's not uncommon for things to get lost in translation; all of these theories are certainly possible. It's also possible that Cleopas, Cleophas, and Clopas were the same person. Mary could have also been the infamous "Other Mary." Some have also interpreted Mary as the mother of Jesus and Clopas was her second husband.[26]

Cleopas and Mary — It's also possible that the companion was Mary, and Cleopas was her husband. Luke says they ask Jesus to "stay with us" which means that they seem to be living together; it's also possible that they are just related and sharing a home.

Jesus uses many devices to teach—and what follows is indeed a teaching—the device he uses here starts by him quizzing the men. He wants the men to explain what they think had just happened.

If this is a quiz, the two men failed it. If you are a follower of Jesus Christ, and you just heard he rose from the dead

---

[26] Joseph having died.

and fulfilled everything he said he would, and you're walking on the road back home, then wouldn't you be talking about how amazing it is?! These two men basically tell Jesus all of that—but they miss the part about this being prophecy fulfilled. In reality, the two men are really confused. Like, seriously confused. Their great teacher has just been hung on a cross, and now there are reports about his body missing. It makes sense that they draw the logical conclusion and probably imagine that someone has taken his body.

Jesus—the kind and patient teacher—isn't so kind and patient here. He calls them fools. He's not subtle about it. He doesn't hold anything back. We often think of Jesus as a tolerable person, but he doesn't seem very tolerable here. There are a lot of reasons for this, but the one here seems to be because Jesus expects better of us. He's patient with the unbeliever, but when we confess with our lips that we believe in Jesus—when we follow him and trust in him—and then we act like these disciples and really let him down, he's not afraid to call us on our poor behaviors, or acts. He's going to call us fools. And even though Christ is forgiving, when he does this, it stings a little.

But he doesn't spend the next several hours lecturing them. He spends the time with them to make it right—to make them see as they should see. When our hearts are open, God will make it right—he will help us to see what he wants us to see.

Let's rewind for a minute. Jesus is back from the dead. He's suffered. And he's gone through what we can only imagine is some kind of terrible experience. If I came back from the dead, I'd probably start with, "Have I got something to tell you!" And then I'd proceed with this magical experience I just went through. So, you can only imagine what's about to follow this cringe-worthy scolding is going to be quite a lesson. And it is. But it's not what you might expect.

It's a Bible study.

Jesus often used parables to prove a point. He could be quite poetic in his teachings. But not now—when you'd expect him to be his most poetic, he's actually the most Jewish.

There is a place for parables, but right now the most important thing that needs to be taught is not what has transpired, rather what has been fulfilled. The prophecy of the Old Testament has come to pass.

Jesus turns to Moses—and all the prophets that follow. In Luke 24:27, it says, "And beginning with Moses and all the Prophets, he explained to them what was said in all the Scriptures concerning himself." (NIV) So we don't know what exactly was said, but we do know what this Bible study was about. We don't get to know what the two men were thinking—how they were reacting, because this story isn't about them.

Beginning with Moses, the Jewish people entered their most longstanding covenant with God. It's the one that introduced God's people to some of his greatest hits: The Ten Commandments, David and Goliath, Daniel and the Den of Lions—the covenant was a hit-making machine. But in between all these greatest hits were prophets who prophesied that something greater was coming: a new covenant. And with that new covenant: a Messiah. And this was the turning point that Bible study gave the men: *that Messiah had come.*

You would think at this point the eyes of the men would be open; but, again, that does not appear to be the case; they invite Jesus to fellowship with them inside their house, but they are not ready to say this man is their Lord.

So, in they walk into their home, and it's a classic, "Hey guys! Guess who's coming to dinner?!"

When you have a guest over for dinner, then you are—in a word—hospitable. That's not without reason. People have been doing this hospitable act for ages. They did it one hundred years ago; they did it two thousand years ago. So, what we should be seeing is these men and others in their home treating Jesus as a guest.

But in Luke 24:30, it tells us that as they ate, Jesus took the bread, "gave thanks, broke it and began to give it to them." That may not seem unusual, but this is not what a guest does. This is what a host should be doing.

Jesus is serving when he should be served. There's a lesson there that's often overlooked; everything Jesus does is to teach us what we should do. He's not afraid to serve when he's supposed to be served to—and neither should we.

Jesus has different ways of revealing his nature post-Resurrection—to Mary it was when he said her name that she finally opened her eyes and saw him. To these two men, it's the communion. There are lots of theories about this. One of the more popular ones is as Jesus broke the bread, the disciples looked down and saw his hands and the nail marks and immediately knew who it was. I don't think so. Remember, the Bible says they were "kept" from recognizing him.

Communion is one of the holiest sacraments you can take. Sometimes people take it for granted today. But if we're going to be Biblical about it, you don't take the sacrament until you've made things right with God.[27] You don't come before God while you still have an enemy you have not forgiven or a wrong you have not made right.

These disciples were "kept" from seeing Jesus standing right in front of them because they had to make things right; the communion symbolized them coming to the realization that Jesus wasn't just a great teacher—he was the son of God—the Messiah. Once they break bread, they are "kept" no more from being blinded.

But what happens next is key to this revelation. Jesus leaves. He doesn't say, "So now you get it—finally!" He doesn't proceed with more teaching. He leaves. Jesus knows how to make an exit! He leaves with the disciples' mouths hanging—with them thirsty for more. He leaves with the disciples on fire.

The disciples are burning up with the Spirit after this moment. They don't wait until the sun comes up to tell others what they heard—they take off to tell the others. And remember, this is pre-Edison. There are no lights on the paths. And these are not the safest roads. But none of that matters.

---

[27] 1 Corinthians 11:28

What's the Deal with Communion?

Have you ever really thought about communion?

The history of communion can be both complicated and messy. Putting aside how often it should be celebrated, there's the question of wine or grape juice; the Bible says wine, but prohibition made that complicated—Welch's Food Inc., the multi-billion-dollar beverage company, was started with the sole intention of providing grape juice to churches. Many theologians (mostly Protestant) went to great lengths to explain how Jesus *really* meant grape juice when he said wine. The theological question of grape juice or wine is just for starters—others have argued whether we should use one cup or small individual cups; and don't get me started on the argument for what kind of bread should be used.

The question is, why is communion even important? The Bible certainly talks about it, but Jesus never gives the direct command: thou shalt break bread once a month—unless thy bread is discounted at the supermarket, and then break it before it's moldy.

One of the very few arguments for the frequency of communion is Acts 20:7: "On the first day of the week we came together to break bread. Paul spoke to the people and, because he intended to leave the next day, kept on talking until midnight." (NIV) This seems to tell us that Christians were doing this weekly, but other instances seem to argue that they were doing it even more regularly—whenever they were together.

The reality is, however, when we argue about the frequency—or about what drink should be used or if it should be in one cup or several—we're probably are missing the point of what communion is. Jesus tells his disciples to take communion to remember him. Are we going to remember him less if we don't eat a piece of bread dipped in wine or juice every week? Probably not. But when we think of it like that, then we're being selfish—communion isn't about us: it's about the community of believers. We come together to take it—to fellowship. Jesus broke bread and gave us perhaps one of the most telling theological lessons of what church should be: a place to come together and remember what Jesus Christ did for us.

The church I was raised in had a communion table in the center of the church—the pulpit was to the side of it; thinking back on this arrangement, it's clear what the point was: communion should be front and center. Communion is the church. And church isn't the place we go on Sunday. Church is the place we go to fellowship with other believers. Realistically, communion should be taken whenever we are with believers: at Bible studies, at church dinners, anywhere. It's the sacrament we should get most excited for. It shouldn't be a ritual—it should be a living sacrament that we celebrate and rejoice over.

# # #

Curiously, it's while they are *walking* that Jesus teaches them that they need to walk by faith and not by sight.

It's in the unexpected that we can see God's beauty. God is not revealing what man knows—he's showing us a glimpse of a reality that is beyond our understanding: a world where the unexpected in man's eyes starts to make sense.

Christ is around us, but we don't always see him. He's standing next to us in our joys and trials—next to us in all things. He's next to us now. But we don't recognize his presence until we need him. He knows when we need him.

And just like these men, he doesn't linger when he helps us. He gives us just enough to get us through, but he also makes us want more—hungry to feel his presence again—which isn't to say he leaves us: he's always there. It's in these men that Christ begins to show the drive that should be in all Christians—that would certainly be in his disciples; it's what will keep the disciples going when any other human who was not under the power of God would stop—and it's what keeps us going as well.

For these men, what stopped them from really experiencing Christ is not understanding the Resurrection. Once Jesus taught them about it, they were cleansed and they were ready to receive him. Jesus knows us personally, but before we accept that, he wants us to come to him ready to receive that—not to come to him while we're still holding grudges, or anger.

Jesus doesn't call us to receive him with a perfect heart—the fact that he knows us personally means that he understands we are coming to him with struggles and flaws—and he's going to get us through that. But our heart still needs to be clean. He has to be ready and open to receive what's going to come next.

UNSTOPPABLE CHRISTIANS

When it comes to fathers of the early church, you can't get any sexier than Augustine of Hippo. His timeless yawn-inducing works *The City of God* and *Confessions* have been required readings[28] for pretty much every seminary student since publication.

The mighty Hippo had his own encounter with God—though not on a path—and, in classic Augustine style, more bizarre than what the Emmaus Duo encountered.

Before you hear about the encounter, it's best to hear about Hippo's life prior. Prior to being one of the original kings of theology, Hippo was best known for being a horrible person. He was born to a pagan father and Christian mother. As a young adult, he became a follower and student of Manichaeism.[29]

---

[28] Or at the very least, required to purchase and put on bookshelf and said to have read and been greatly influenced by.

[29] A now forgotten religion that, at the time, was the main competition to Christianity; it taught the conflict of the spiritual world and the material world.

Hippo got his Roman on at the age of 19 and began a relationship that resulted in the birth of his only son, Adeodatus; after years of being with his lover, Hippo realized it was time to man up and marry a 10-year-old. Don't get too grossed out by that—he was fully prepared to wait until she was 12[30] to take her as his wife.

A funny thing happened on his way to marrying his child-bride. Hippo, then 31, had been struggling because he felt his sexual desires had gotten in the way of his thinking; about this time, he met a bishop who showed him how surrendering to God could help him conquer all of this. It was a lot to take in, and he decided to chill for a spell under a tree; it was here that he heard a child's voice singing, "Take it and read it; take it and read it." Nearby was Paul's Letter to the Romans—the verse he happened to see first: "Let us behave decently, as in the daytime, not in orgies and drunkenness, not in sexual immorality and debauchery, not in dissension and jealousy. Rather, clothe yourself with the Lord Jesus Christ." (Romans 13:13-14)

On the evening of Easter, Hippo was baptized, ditched his child-bride, became a celibate priest, and was one of the most unstoppable Christians who ever lived.

---

[30] Marrying age back then.

THREE

....

THIRD TIME'S A CHARM?

T hird time's a charm. Finally, Jesus is going to get up close and personal with the people who knew him best.

But first, I must interrupt this regularly scheduled broadcast / chapter with breaking news: Peter. Because this appearance isn't *really* the first time he appeared to a disciple. As mentioned in Chapter 2, there is a vague reference to what has been aptly dubbed a "secret meeting" with Peter, which happened before Jesus met with Cleopas and his companion.

We know very little about the meeting. It's referenced only twice: "It is true! The Lord has risen and has appeared to Simon." (Luke 24:34) and "He appeared to Cephas,[31] and then the Twelve" (1 Corinthians 15:5).

So, if there's little known about it, we should just write it off, right? That would be careless, because even if we don't

---

[31] Or Peter.

know all the details of the meeting, there's a lesson to be learned.

Here's what is obvious: Peter is the disciple who has been on fire for Jesus; he's the rock star of the group of twelve. But when the time comes for Peter to step it up and lead, Peter falls flat on his face and fails miserably. Not only did he just sort of back away and not support Jesus during his trial, but he outright disowned Jesus. But it's worse than that—he disowns him not once, not twice, but three times.

So, Peter is flying low.

When he hears Jesus is alive, there's obviously joy, but one can also imagine Peter feels as if he's been punched in the gut. He's heard good news, but then he probably realizes that his previous actions now have more substantial consequences then he ever imagined.

Still, Peter's passion is still there; when the Marys report the empty tombs, Peter sprints to the tomb to see it with his own eyes. It's worth noting that Peter likely wasn't fired up because he thought it was all true—that Jesus Christ had risen from the dead like he said he would. Luke 24:12 explains, "But they did not believe the women, because their words seemed to them like nonsense." The disciples, at this point, probably just thought that Jesus' body had been stolen or removed from the tomb.

So, Peter and John dash to the tomb. And this is where it gets a little vague. At some point after this, Jesus appears to Peter. What happened? Something.

Did Jesus speak to Peter? Did he just appear to him? Was it quick? John later gives the account of Jesus reinstating

Jesus Ascended. What Does That Mean?

Peter, so one can easily speculate that this encounter was likely brief—something to make Peter know it's true, so he can slowly begin to come to terms and wrestle with it. But that's just speculation.

What we do know is this was a personal encounter. Unlike the first three appearances, where there are lessons for everyone to take in, this encounter is for Peter. The reader, in these instances, is not meant to learn anything other than the fact that it happened.

So, what's the lesson? What could we possibility get out of this vague and highly personal encounter? When we think about the reinstatement of Peter, we think of this immediate transformation. This character who changes at the snap of a finger. And that's sometimes how it can seem in our own life—people expect immediate change. But God didn't expect Peter to change overnight and he doesn't expect you to either.

God planted a seed in Peter here, and he let that seed grow in him for the next several days; so, when it's time for the forgiveness scene that most of us know to happen, he's ready for it. If there's something in our life that we need to change—or perhaps just an area that we need to grow in— God is already planting seeds. We're changing even if we haven't had this epiphany moment yet. And one day we'll be changed, and it may seem sudden, but God had been working in our hearts all along.

The Rule of Threes

Jesus rises from the dead in three days. Peter denounces Jesus three times. So far there's been three major lessons that Jesus has taught. There's a whole lot of threes going on. But we shouldn't read anything into that, right? The Bible is a multi-dimensional book. You've heard of 3D? 4D Perhaps? What about ∞D? That's the Bible. The dimensions are infinite and you should read into *everything*. It's the only book where you can have 12 people read a passage and get 12 completely different perspectives.

So, three? What gives? When three is used in the Bible, it's to signify completeness.

God is composed of—or completed—by three beings: The Father, The Son, and The Holy Spirit.

Before the flood—before the covenant God formed with Abraham—there were three Patriarchs: Abel, Enoch, and Noah.

And speaking of this covenant with Abraham? There's three more Patriarchs that come with that covenant: Abraham, Isaac, and Jacob.

It's hard to measure just how long Jesus' ministry lasted, but the Gospel of John references three Passovers over the course of Jesus' ministry; this has been used to say his ministry lasted three years. So, three again, could be used, to say that it took Jesus three years to complete his ministry.

The New Testament is God's new covenant with man.

There are 27 books in the New Testament. That's 27 books to complete the book that completes God's new covenant. 27. So where's the three in that? 3^3.

The book of Revelations—that weird book and the one that ends the Bible, which has been widely interpreted and often widely misunderstood—it defines God as, "which is, and which was, and which is to come." (Revelation 1:4, NIV)

When you see three in the Bible, ask yourself this question: has something just been completed? Because often, the answer is yes and there's something to be learned from it.

#   #   #

And now, we return to our regularly scheduled chapter / broadcast—the moment we've all been waiting for—the most epic guess who's coming to dinner *ever*. Even more epic than the one he had with Cleopas and that other guy. Here we begin to see how Christ can really shape and change us when we are open to his power.

We've all been there—that awkward dinner where sitting across from us is the person we perhaps don't want to see, or perhaps the person we are just surprised to see. But what if that person is Jesus?[32] That would be pretty cool—certainly surprising. But let's add some perspective to this, because, unlike us, who know about the Resurrection, these disciples are still in shock and grief mode. They are confused. This

---

[32] Quick! Hide the pork and make dinner kosher.

guy they've been following for the past three years is suddenly gone—and more than that, he isn't what they thought he was: The Messiah. Because if he was the Messiah, then he wouldn't be gone—he would have become a mighty ruler.

The disciples are in a worrisome state. Unlike the disciples who will later go as far as to die in the name of Jesus Christ, these guys are gathered together afraid that any second the Jewish leaders will break down their door and arrest them. It doesn't say why they're afraid this will happen, but the most likely reason is the body of Christ is gone and the Jewish leaders think that they took it to start a revolution.

There was *so much* that these disciples needed to learn. Don't fret: they're going to learn it quickly.

So here they are. Alone. Afraid. Confused.

Jesus suddenly appears to them, and both Luke 24:36 and John 20:19 record Jesus as saying, "Peace be with you." (NIV)

This is the part where you expect the disciples to run to him! To hug him! To weep in joy! To worship him! But things, as you should be learning by now, don't happen as you'd expect. The disciples, instead of being elated, are outright terrified. In fact, they think he is a ghost.

This could have been Jesus' first teaching opportunity; he could have said, "A ghost?! Are you kidding me? I told you exactly what was going to happen and now that it's happened, you still don't believe? Seriously?! Come on guys!" But he's sensitive to their fear.

Jesus Ascended. What Does That Mean?

Perhaps you've heard a fire-and-brimstone preacher—a preacher who scares the Jesus into you by telling you if you don't believe, you'll eternally be burned and tortured more than you even know. And perhaps that works for some people. But what Jesus shows here is that fear doesn't work for most people; he's showing that God is sensitive to our fears and doubts. He's not going to try and scare us into believing. He's going to let belief come naturally.

So, Jesus is calm, and his first order of business is to prove that he is indeed *not* a ghost. He tells them to touch him and feel that he has flesh and bones.

Jesus is no ghost. He proves this here. But why is he no ghost? Why is it so important to show that he is flesh and bones? Even if Jesus could come back as a ghost after three days, and appear to people, then that would be pretty cool, right? God is spiritual. So why can't Jesus be spiritual? Why can't he just be a floating being that comes and gives peace to people? Surely you don't need flesh and bones to do that.

Could Jesus Christ have returned as a ghost? Would that *really* have been wrong? It's a fair question, but to answer it, first it's important to consider what the Bible actually says about ghosts.

First, ghosts are real. They're Biblical. In Samuel 28:1-19, Saul goes to a medium of Endor to call up the spirit of Samuel. The medium, or witch, is able to do it. But, it should be pointed out, she was able to do it because God allowed it—and things did not go so well for Saul because of his carelessness. There are other instances of ghosts in the Bible. Theologians have lots of theories about them; many would say they are evil spirits—not actually the deceased person. But what is clear is that God does not use ghosts to communicate with us.[33]

So, for Jesus to be a ghost, it would be contradicting everything God has taught believers to think about the spirit world—which is not to mess with it. Getting Old Testament for a minute, God revealed his message through himself; he didn't get some zombie kid from down the street to give it to them. To give this final teaching to the disciples, it needed to be from God Himself giving the message.

Jesus is God; but Jesus is also man. He has two natures. God manifested himself into the body of a man to fully prove that he understands man—to suffer as we suffer. In the Ascension, he takes this body to Heaven, but he's not gone yet.

Once Jesus shows them his hands, it clicks. They get it. Relieved, Jesus admits he's hungry. But is he really? Sure, he's just been in a dark tomb the past three days, but is hunger really what's going on here? It's important to note that "he ate it in their presence." (Luke 24:43, NIV) It doesn't say the disciples eat with him. This isn't a communion act, because they aren't joining in. Jesus is again demonstrating for them that he is the real deal—only a man will do that; visions don't do that; ghost don't do that; dreams don't do that. They've just touched him, but he needs them to know

---

[33] Sorry, Bruce Willis fans...*The Sixth Sense* was *not* based on a true story.

without a shadow of doubt that what they are seeing is Jesus Christ in the flesh.

The disciples had certainly heard the accounts by now of Jesus' appearance, but they were likely making excuses for them—the person was just seeing things and is in shock; but now they have proof—and missing fish to go along with that proof.

Now that the disciples have absolutely no reason to doubt, he gets down to business: it's time for a teaching.

Jesus isn't too hard on the disciples, but he does make it clear that this teaching shouldn't be anything new to them; in Luke 24:44, Jesus says, "This is what I told you while I was still with you." (NIV) Interpretation: "Come on guys! What part of *I'm the Messiah* did you not understand?!"

The disciples probably had their heads down at this point; they messed up. They should have known. John 20:21 says that Jesus said again "Peace be with you!" He knew what they were thinking, and he's telling them now that it's okay—they are forgiven: God is with them.

The Book of Acts tell us that the Holy Spirit descended on the Apostles at Pentecost. That's true. But it could really be argued that Pentecost begins on this night. Both Luke and John tell us that Jesus opened the minds of the disciples, but John 20:22 goes deeper and says he told them to "Receive the Holy Spirit." (NIV)

This passage is the most telling teaching that has happened so far. In every instance that Jesus reveals himself, minds are being opened, but it is with John that we see what happens when minds are opened.

Consider for a moment, the passage: Receive the Holy Spirit.

What does that mean to you?

It's unfortunate that in the mad dash of the world that we often are so focused on getting people to believe in God that we don't consider that a person must also receive God. Just because you go to some Bible crusade and go to the front of the church to say you believe in Jesus Christ doesn't mean that you are saved.

A person can believe in Jesus Christ—they can believe in God—they can even obey the commandments—and not be saved. That may seem a little unorthodox, but it's only because we are often taught a very watered-down version of the Bible. But all of this is very Biblical.

In Acts 8, the author tells the story of a sorcerer named Simon, who became a believer after he heard about Christ from Phillip. But that word "believer" is important here, because the passage goes on to say in Acts 8:14-17:

When the apostles in Jerusalem heard that Samaria had accepted the word of God, they sent Peter and John to Samaria. When they arrived, they prayed for the new believers there that they might receive the Holy Spirit, because the Holy Spirit had not yet come to any of them; they had simply been baptized in the name of the Lord Jesus.

Salvation is really a two-step process; sometimes these steps happen together, and sometimes it takes time for the second to happen. Perhaps the best verse on what salvation is is Romans 10:9 which says that "If you declare with your mouth, 'Jesus is Lord,' and believe in your heart that God raised him from the dead, you will be saved." The verse shows the two steps to salvation:

Step One: Believe outwardly.

Step Two: Receive inwardly.

This process isn't unique to you and me—this is something that applies to even the disciples and early believers. For the past three some odd years, these disciples had been following Jesus. They believed in him.

In Luke 24:44, Jesus teaches them, "Everything must be fulfilled that is written about me in the Law of Moses, the Prophets and the Psalms." (NIV) And again, they believe. But they haven't received.

When Jesus stood in front of them—when he revealed himself to Mary(s), the man and the companion, and finally to the disciples—they each had their eyes opened. And they believed. But they had not received.

With the disciples, the reader is seeing for the first time more concretely what the next forty days will be about: receiving the Holy Spirit.

Many times, people accept Christ, and they're on fire—they're ready to go out and preach the good news! They're willing to die for the cross. These are exactly the type of people God wants, right? Not so fast. Because Christ doesn't say, "Okay boys! Have at 'em!" Luke 24:49 clarifies that while they will receive the Holy Spirit (i.e. what the Father has promised in verse 49), they are to "stay in the city until you have been clothed with the power from on high." What does that mean? It means they're fired up, but that doesn't mean that they are ready.

When we receive the Holy Spirit, we must pause and consider it. Pray. Mediate. Be still. Be silent. God wants us to spread the Word; he wants us to go out into the world. But he also wants us to be close to him. The disciples were no doubt fired up, but first they needed to connect with God. They had a relationship with God on Earth, and now they would need to understand what it means to have a relationship with God in Heaven.

There would come a time to go out into the world. Jesus tells them they will go out to the world and "If you forgive anyone's sins, their sins are forgiven; if you do not forgive them, they are not forgiven." (John 20:23)

That passage is easy to misinterpret. In fact, it can be used as ammo to condemn a person who you think is not acting in a manner that is…like you. This verse isn't about believers getting to have the rule of condemnation—about telling people who suffer from any kind of sin that they are going to burn in hell.

To be clear: only God has the ability to forgive. Man has only the ability to preach God's forgiveness.

So, what's going on here? Jesus is not telling them that they get to be judges. And he's not addressing each person personally. What's lost in translation is there is a plural word being used; in other words, he is saying as a community of believers (i.e., the church). What does the church have the ability to do? Tell people that God loves them, and that God forgives them.

He's telling them that through the Spirit, they can go out to the world and tell people that if they believe in the message and receive the Spirit, then they are forgiven—because this is what God has already said. He's not giving them the ability to invent or interpret what is right and wrong. Right and wrong here is unique to only one thing: believing in the Message.

When it says that if "they don't forgive, then they are not forgiven," it's not saying, "aren't you powerful! You have the ability to decide." It's saying if you tell someone about the Message of Christ and they reject it, then they are not forgiven.

\#　　\#　　\#

Christ has now had three documented encounters,[34] and the order of when and why they happened seems clearer. First, Jesus appeared to individuals; it was personal. Second, Jesus appeared to a small company. And third, Jesus appeared to an assembled community. The order is showing how the Gospel is effectively spread: first, believers talk with a person at an individual, intimate level; then at a slightly larger level—with one or two others who can help us work through our doubts; and finally, in the fellowship of a larger gathering where it all comes together.

In the first encounter, Jesus is the friend. Just as when we first believed, it was probably because a friend came to us and told us at the most personal level what we believed. In the next encounter, Jesus is a teacher; and this, too, is really the next level most of us take—we heard it from a friend and

---

[34] Not counting Peter, which is referenced, but for which the details are not documented.

it sounds pretty solid, but we want to go and hear more. Finally, in the last encounter, Jesus is the Master; we believe and now it's time for us to go beyond belief and receive him, and be called to be sent out to proclaim the good news for the world.

UNSTOPPABLE CHRISTIANS

Preachers today don't have it so bad. At megachurches, they have speakers in places larger than some Cineplex's; they have jumbo screens to emphasize their points; some even have teleprompters with pages of notes.

Preachers today are no match for one of the greatest preachers who ever lived: Charles Spurgeon.

Spurgeon's sermons were just as legendary as the way he executed them. Think of the largest church you've been to. Then think bigger. Then think, this guy's preaching with no mic. Once you're there, then you can start to have an idea for the way Spurgeon preached.

By the age of 22, Spurgeon had grown a dwindling church to a church with thousands of regular congregants; he also had published a collection of sermons. His sermons were so popular, they were published and distributed in print weekly.

Spurgeon, at the cost of losing followers and having a decline in the sale of his sermons, vocally opposed slavery.

It was not uncommon for more than 10,000 people to

show up and hear him preach. At his largest gathering (at London's Crystal Palace), 23,654 were recorded showing up—and he preached to them with no microphone.[35]

While Spurgeon did typically prepare his sermons in advance, he only went to the pulpit with one notecard that had an outline; with this short outline, he would preach for about forty minutes.

Spurgeon's sons, while never reaching the popularity of their father, also became pastors.

---

[35] Microphones weren't widely available until after his death.

FOUR

....

DOUBTS AND ALL

N othing exciting ever happened at my college. So, when I heard a real-time Hollywood movie was be- ing shot on campus, I was more than a little excited. David Duchovny was there! And Ivan Reitman was direct- ing it.[36]

But I found out too late.

By the time I got to the shooting location, it was all packed up and only the guys packing everything up were there.

I missed out.

My missing out was a big deal at the time—albeit a nerdy missing out—but nothing compared to Thomas. Thomas had history's most epic "missed out." He missed out on seeing Jesus.

The Bible doesn't say why. I imagine how much more crushing it would be when we discover where Thomas was. How would you feel if you stayed home from church be-

---

[36] It was called *Evolution*.

cause it was the season finale of *Game of Thrones* and this was the night that Jesus showed up to give a sermon? I'm pretty sure Thomas wasn't watching *Game of Thrones*, but perhaps it was worse—perhaps he missed out because he was too cowardly to be associated with the disciples. Perhaps he was in hiding.

We don't know the whole story; still, there's a lesson not only in Thomas' doubt, but what prevented Thomas from being with the other disciples. I think Thomas was in a place where we've all been: a place of comfort. Jesus was a great teacher, and it was great while it lasted, but now he's gone, and Thomas is going to get out while he still could.

When the disciples come to him and say that Jesus is alive, he doubts entirely. But is it doubt alone that is causing his resistance? Or is it the fact that if it's true, then he'll have to maybe do something about it?

We've all had those moments when we're driving down the highway and we see a homeless person begging for money. And we've all had the thought: they're probably not even homeless—they probably will just spend the money on booze and drugs. I've had the thought more times than I'd care to admit. Realistically, I don't want to know where the money will go. I don't want to know their story—that it will actually go to feed their child, or give them shelter, or simply just feed them; I want to know that it will go to booze and drugs. I want to know this because it's far easier to just believe they are bad people or that they deserve to be where they are.

When faced with reality it's far easier to make excuses than to face truth. It's far easier to just deny. If I went to an atheist and said, "God is real!" for many it's far easier to just deny it and not ask me why I believe this. If they deny it, then they can just go on believing it's not true; but if they ask me why, there's a chance I might be able to prove it—and that could knock them out of their comfort zone.

So, when Thomas hears from the other disciples that they have seen Jesus alive and well, he takes the easy—comfortable—path. He says, "Unless I see the nail marks in his hands and put my finger where the nails were, and put my hand into his side, I will not believe." (John 20:25, NIV) The fact that Thomas wants to put his hands where the nail marks were, seems to imply that Thomas didn't doubt that they saw "something" but he probably just thought they were a little delusional—it had, after all, been an emotional few days.

Time goes by. I imagine Thomas has gotten pretty pouty. The disciples are probably going on and on about how miraculous it is that Jesus appeared. And he's the odd man out. He's still doubting, for sure, but he's also feeling alone. These guys he's had a great bond with for the past several years are changing, and he's just the same old Thomas.

As the disciples are going joyfully around, there's probably something else that Thomas is feeling: empty. He picked feeling comfortable. He picked making an excuse. And that didn't get him anything but bitterness and loneliness.

#   #   #

Jesus Ascended. What Does That Mean?

My wife and I started going to a new church a few years back. It was big—the kind with plush seats and cushy backs. It was nice. But it was all too easy to get comfortable; to just recline in the seat, listen to the message, and go home. It didn't take long for us to look at easy other and say, "I don't really feel anything here."

It wasn't the church's fault. It was our fault. A Sunday message isn't going to change you. It's not even going to transform you. Think about the Sermon on the Mount; think about any of Jesus' sermons. Sorry to interrupt you here, Kanye, but Jesus is the greatest preacher of *all* time! But it wasn't the sermons that transformed his disciples. It was when they combined those sermons with their actions. When my wife and I started volunteering, then our hearts changed and the church wasn't quite so comfortable. It was what we needed.

So, Thomas is sitting here, and he's comfortably empty. He has heard the greatest sermons from the greatest preacher, but that's not enough. Because if you hear the sermons but don't act on them, it's meaningless.

Then out of nowhere Jesus comes and after telling them "Peace be with you!" he doesn't waste any time. He goes straight to Thomas and says, "Put your finger here; see my hands. Reach out your hand and put it into my side. Stop doubting and believe." (John 20:26-27, NIV)

You have to wonder if Thomas wanted a take-back at this point. I know I would have. If Jesus stood in front of me, and said, "Go ahead—stick your fingers in the nail holes," I would probably take a few steps back and say, "I'm good,

Lord—I was just kidding about that whole finger through the nail marks thing—that's a little too morbid for me!"

John doesn't record what happened—if Thomas actually touched him. But that's not important. He could have just stared dumbfounded for several minutes. What's important is what Thomas said, "My Lord and my God!" (John 20:28)—Thomas believed.

This encounter is actually a first for Jesus—the first encounter Mary realizes it's Jesus when he says her name; the second, it's during a sacrament; and the third, it's in his greeting. Here, it's the marks of his suffering that make it real; it's as if Jesus is saying "Thomas, I don't want you to believe in me—I want you to believe in what I did for you; I want you to look at my hands and understand my suffering."

As Thomas' heart is probably sinking as he begins to realize this, Jesus hits him a little harder by basically saying, "Shame on you for not believing."[37]

When people think of the Bible, they think about that happy ending—about Jesus rising. Who wouldn't celebrate that! But when you think about the forty days, there aren't a lot of happy endings. There's no happy ending here. The chapter ends and Thomas doesn't get a final hug it up with Jesus.

In the last chapter of the book, we'll see what happened to each of the disciples. Thomas may have not gotten his happy ending in John, but he was definitely on fire for God.

---

[37] John 20:29: "Because you have seen me, you have believed; blessed are those who have not seen and yet have believed." (NIV)

\# \# \#

Stigmatastic!

People have been forever fascinated with the wounds on Christ's hands.

In Galatians 6:17, Paul says, "I bear on my body the marks of Jesus." Interpretation? He was probably beaten pretty badly. He uses a Greek word to describe it: Stigmata. The meaning of that word is linked to a marking or tattoo.

If the word "stigmata" sounds even a little familiar to you, then you might be a Catholic. This has become the term used to describe a Christian who has some kind of bodily mark or sore in the place that Jesus would have had his nails.

Francis of Assisi—a Catholic friar—gets credit for being the first person to ever record this phenomenon. It happened in 1224. He would not be the last. Throughout history, several people have experienced stigmata.

The last notable case was Padre Pio.

Unlike Assisi, who didn't live in a time when these sorts of things could be examined and further debunked, Pio died in 1968. Doctors examined him—some even taking X-rays. They couldn't figure it out. It was unexplained.

The marks stayed with him for 50 years. What else could have caused this? Some have speculated carbolic acid, which Pio did make a request for; but this was commonly used for sterilization, and Pio frequently administer injections to children to fight off the Spanish flu.

After 50 years, Pio died; they came for his body, and guess what they found? Or perhaps I should say, guess what they didn't find? The stigmata. It had completely disappeared.

Jesus didn't want Thomas to believe just because. He doesn't want any of us to. If a person grows up never learning about God, Jesus isn't going to stand before them and say, "How dare you for not believing! Shame on you!" Blind belief wasn't Thomas' folly.

Thomas' folly was that he heard the witness of the other disciples and he didn't believe. He got comfortable.

God puts opportunities in front of us all the time. And we make excuses. That's what Thomas did. He was given the opportunity to believe, and he said, "You know what? I'm good! If God wanted me to do this, he would have come to me too."

God, as it turned out, did come to Thomas. And it hurt. He came to him and said, "Thomas, I did tell you to do this! And you didn't do it."

God loves us. He forgives us. But when he gives you an opportunity—when he gives you witness and says, "Here it is all laid out" and you don't take it—he's going to come knocking.

Jesus didn't come to Thomas and say, "Because you didn't believe, I'm giving you cancer, or I'm taking your first child, or any other afflictions." Jesus came to Thomas and said: I'm disappointed in you.

The moral of the story isn't to show a happy ending. It's to show we can, and do, disappoint God. Disappointment is an emotional punishment that stays with us and makes us not want to do that again.

I misbehaved as a child. My parents, though they regret this now, would bring out the hand and bring on the spanking. They regret it because it didn't work. What they realized was if you want to correct the behavior of a child, then you have to affect them on an emotional level, not a physical level. A spanking stings—for a few seconds. And then it goes away.

I kept on misbehaving because it was worth it. It was worth those few seconds of sting for the glory of being a brat. But when my parents started using a different tactic—when they started saying what you are doing is disappointing us—then my behavior started to change. I didn't want to misbehave because letting someone down is far worse than the sting of a physical swat.

I would love to read Thomas' memoir, because I know this chapter of his book is the one that defined his life. I imagine it's something he talked about his entire ministry; he would probably preach multiple sermons about picking convenience and comfort over living for God. About how comfort gave him temporary happiness, but not fulfillment.

The disciples weren't chosen because they were great people; they were chosen for being ordinary people. They were chosen because a part of us lives in them. They had the same doubts that we would have had. They had the same flaws that we would have had. He picked them to show you that if they can do extraordinary things, then we can as well.

Jesus is turning these men into unstoppable Christians. When we let God into our hearts—when we invite him in and do more than just say that we believe—when we act on the belief—then we become unstoppable ourselves.

UNSTOPPABLE CHRISTIANS

Doubt happens. It happened to Thomas. It happens to all of us. Unless you happen to be so on fire—so unstoppable—that you just don't have time to do it. Robert Murray M'Cheyne was of the doubtless variety.

M'Cheyne wasn't the showy type—he didn't want his dear old mom to brag about him knowing the alphabet by the age of four. Any child could learn that. He took it up a step and learned the Greek alphabet. By 14, he was already in college. And by 18, he was ready to begin his career. He was obviously a whiz kid, but he also loved Jesus and decided to become a minister.

M'Cheyne, in addition to being a pastor, also was a poet and writer; he helped launch several mission efforts; and he created one of the most widely used systems at the time for reading the Bible (following it, people would read the New Testament and Psalms twice a year, and the Old Testament once). It sounds like a very full life, right? It was…right up until his death at the age of 29.

In the short time between graduating college at 18 and his death at 29, M'Cheyne accomplished more than most Christians can say they've accomplished in their entire life.

Doubt can be good. It can even help you grow. But it can almost limit your abilities to spread the Gospel, which is what we are called to do, and that is when doubt can become dangerous.

FIVE

....

THE SEA OF PETER

I like going to New York. It's not exactly exotic, but when I'm there, I get to pretend I'm someone I'm not. I get to get lost in the big city. See the sites. Eat like a local. Take in all the atmosphere. When I'm there, it's like home doesn't even exist. Home is New York.

When I go to New York—or take any vacation for that matter—work doesn't follow me. For a few short days, I can see what life would be like without it.

But I do have a home. And when I get back, I'm often overwhelmed with disappointment. Reality sinks in. Responsibilities are back. The dogs are back. The cats are back. Chores are back. My work life returns. It's like something magical had happened, but then I realize it was all just a dream—I realize the vacation is over.

The disciples had just been on an adventure. They had spent years with Jesus Christ—God in the flesh. And the icing on the cake was that he came back from the dead! It seems like they've had their great awakening. How do you go back to normal after something like that? How does life just go on? Jesus is going to show us what happens next—what happens after we receive him? How does life just go on?

It's in our nature to forget the value of even the impactful things.[38]

Jesus appeared to the disciples, and then life went on. John doesn't record how long it took for life to go on, but in 21:2, it says that Simon Peter said, "I'm going fishing," and a few of the other disciples went with him. It seems odd at first, but fishing is what they knew. It was their job. It was their way of making life go on.

The thing to understand here is that seeing Jesus doesn't make you live for Jesus—it doesn't make you have a relationship with him, and it surely doesn't give you salvation. If you look up from this book and there in front of you is Jesus Christ, and he's going in for a high five: you don't automatically get marked as a disciple of Christ. You're marked as being a witness to something miraculous, but that's about it.

The fact that these disciples had followed Jesus for all those years—the fact that they saw him—none of that gives

---

[38] How many people remember the 2002 Nord-Ost Siege? You should…over 150 people died and nearly 900 were taken hostage. "But that wasn't on American soil, so why should I remember it?" you say? Fine. How about Emmett Till? See how many of your friends remember him. He's the 14-year-old who was lynched in 1955 for "supposedly" flirting with a white woman. The men who murdered him were acquitted of the crime.

them salvation. They are certainly on the path, but they still don't know what it means to have the personal relationship with Jesus that he came to bring.

So, it should not be surprising at all that they're fishing; they're just doing what they thought they were expected to do. But they weren't doing it very well. They didn't catch a single fish.

When Jesus shows up on the shore and calls out to them, it's back to the drawing board—his beloved disciples again have absolutely no idea who it is.

After a formal greeting, Jesus instructs them to toss their net to the right of the boat if they want to catch fish. (John 21:6) Not knowing this was Jesus, it wouldn't have been odd for them to reject the advice. But they followed—perhaps as an act of desperation. And when they did, they caught so many fish, they weren't even able to haul up their net.

It almost seems like a jerk move; one moment they can't catch any fish and the next they are catching so many fish they can't even bring up their net—these guys are losing even when they're winning! But there's a parable going on. This net is exactly what the road ahead will look like—they will become missionaries, and when they follow the instructions of God, their nets will be full of believers.

In Luke 5:10, Jesus has just performed a very similar miracle when he calls his first disciples and he tells Peter, "Don't be afraid, from now on you will fish for people." Peter no doubt remembers this miracle, and will eventually see the connection and understand that this man on the edge of the sea is Jesus.

The Bible is full of bookends—stories that come around full circle and complete perfectly. In Matthew 4:18-19, Jesus stands beside the Sea of Galilee and he calls two of his disciples, Peter and Andrew. And here we are again. Jesus stands beside the Sea of Galilee and he's about to ask his disciples to take the next step—not just to follow him, but to spread his name to the world. It's fitting.

And it's this bookend, full-circle story that perhaps makes Peter jump in the water; Peter was able to walk on water the first time. That's not the case here, but it's interesting that John takes note of who saw Jesus first—John did.[39] Peter is full of energy and passion, but John appears to be the thinker of the group. And Jesus loves them both equally.

While Peter is throwing all his passion into getting to Jesus as quick as humanly possible, John and others are towing in the net full of fish. When you look at the church, you see all sorts, and none are better than the others—they all are needed to make the church work. Peter is the charismatic one who expresses his faith more outwardly at times than others—and you need that. But then you have John, and he's on the boat realizing that they need people to stay with the boat or they'll lose all this food they just caught.

When they arrive on shore, they see that there's already a fire burning and food waiting. Jesus is showing once again that he's still a servant. He's did something truly remarkable

---

[39] John 21:7

and it would be hard to blame him if he stood on the shore with his arms in the air shouting "Worship me!" But he's showing the disciples that even in his resurrected state that he is a servant. He's giving them an example to follow.

All this begs the question: why the fish? Why did he help them catch all this fish when he already had a feast prepared? Maybe Jesus caught the "what gives?" look on their face because in verse 10 he says, "Bring some of the fish you have just caught." Jesus may have gotten the dinner started, but this is going to be a shared feast.

The passion (and muscle) of Peter shows again because he went right to the fish and carried it to Jesus all by himself. Peter is trying desperately to impress Jesus—and he should be—he is, after all, the guy who completely denied knowing Jesus just a few days before; he's obviously over-joyed to see Jesus, but probably also a little terrified—and definitely still full of guilt.

Let's think about this image for just a minute. Peter single-handedly carries this giant haul of fish. It doesn't say what kind of fish this is, but let's just assume it is one of the most common breeds of fish found in the Sea of Galilee: The Galilaea Tilapia. This particular fish has a maximum weight of about 3.5 pounds. But let's be conservative here; let's just say the fish are 2 pounds on average. That's over 300 pounds of fish that Peter is singlehandedly carrying. That's a lot of guilt that Peter's carrying to be able to muster that kind of strength.

So, here they all are—reunited and it feels so good—except it doesn't. Things are still a bit off. Jesus invites them to eat breakfast with him, and then it goes on to say in verse 12 that none of the disciples "dared ask him, 'Who are you?' They knew it was the Lord." (NIV) Of course it's Jesus! So why does John make it sound so odd that they didn't want to ask who he was? The Bible never explains what Jesus looked like, but John and other authors certainly imply that the resurrected appearance of Jesus was different than the pre-resurrected state. Jesus is not a ghost, but he is not human either—he comes and goes as he pleases.

Jesus again takes the servant role and in verse 13, serves them bread and fish. The disciples probably feel rock bottom right about now. A few chapters back, in John 18, Peter had denied knowing Christ and in John 18:18, right after his denial, it says, "Now the servants[a] and officers had made a charcoal fire, because it was cold, and they were standing and warming themselves. Peter also was with them, standing and warming himself." You have to imagine Peter is staring at that fire and he knows what he did—the guilt inside him is probably burning hotter than those flames. And Thomas is there too—and he knew what he did. They all had denied Jesus in one way or another—and yet Jesus still serves them.

There were probably rivers of tears that night.

# # #

When breakfast is over, Jesus moves on to the main course: Peter. He knows what Peter is going through, but he doesn't say "There, there, Peter—I forgive you. It's ok." He says bluntly in John 21:15, "Simon son of John, do you love me more than these?" (NIV) It's a hard question to hear, but perhaps made worse by the fact that he's calling him "Simon" and not "Peter." Peter means rock. Peter is meant to be the rock—the foundation—that God builds his church on. Jesus is essentially saying that Peter is not that rock…yet.

Peter had previously said he loved Jesus more than the other disciples. But what about now? It should also be noted that Jesus asks the question and uses the Greek word for love "*agapas*"—but when Peter answers that yes, of course he loves him, he uses the Greek word "*phileo*." Both are interpreted as "Love," but one is the giving, unselfish love and the other is the friendly love. So, Jesus is saying, "Peter, do you love me unselfishly?" And Peter replies by saying he loves Jesus like a friend. It's easy to see that Peter is a little more reserved and not so passionate now; he's embarrassed to say he loves Jesus like he did before because he was such a big letdown.

Jesus replies by telling Peter to "Feed my lambs." (Verse 15); the word "my" should be noted here. Jesus is not giving Peter his lambs—he's telling him to take care of them. To tend them.

Jesus asks Peter again if he loves him, and then a third time. And this third time, it really sinks in. Peter denied Jesus three times, and now Jesus is asking if he loves him three times.

Jesus gets Peter fired up, and then he leaves him with two final words: "Follow me!" (Verse 19)

You can't help but wonder what you would reply if Jesus came to you and said, "Follow me." Peter's reply is both comical and relatable. Instead of jumping up and saying, "Heck yeah, I'll follow you!" Peter almost seems downright annoyed and childish! He turns to John and in verse 21 and gives the reply that any 5-year-old gives when they don't like what has been said: "What about him?"

Everyone who's a Christian wants to *believe* that they are on fire for Jesus, but the reality is we're human. When God calls you into action, he knows you are human. Peter needs to process what's been said. It's not an instant call to action—at least for him. Yes, Peter goes on to be the shepherd to the early church—the rock that Jesus predicted he'd become. But first, he needs to digest everything and grow.

Jesus could have smacked him upside the head and said, "Really, Peter?! Grow up!" But he's gentler. In verse 22, he says, "If I want him to remain alive until I return, what is that to you? You must follow me." Jesus is saying "mind your own business"—but he's saying more than that. He's saying every believer has a different destiny. Peter was a competitive guy, but Jesus is trying to humble him. He's showing him that it's not a competition—we are all unique—we all have different paths to God.

It's also important to consider "*You* must follow me." Jesus is telling Peter that it's not about John's decision or Thomas' decision, or anyone else's decision. He can't decide if he's going to follow based on what happens to the next guy. He has to decide because it's a personal choice based solely on his relationship with Jesus Christ. This is telling for all of us. We can't look at other believers to decide if there is a God and if we want to have a relationship with us—we can only examine our own personal relationship and what God has done in our lives.

#   #   #

Jesus is done with his teaching to Peter, but John records more. John gives us a nugget of insight into early Christians in verse 23, "the rumor spread among the believers that this disciple would not die. But Jesus did not say that he would not die." We often look to the Bible and say, "Man, the world would be so much better if people would prescribe to the same moral code they did back then." That's not true. Reality check: people were just as messed up back then as they are today! Perhaps more so! People loved to gossip and add things to the testimony of Christ that simply were not true.

John also tells us in verse 25 there's so much more that happened that isn't in this book—that this was not Jesus' only appearance. For John, for all the disciples and gospel writers, it's the testimony that Christ brought that's important—not the acts that followed when he resurrected. The Resurrection only confirmed that the testimony is true, and so John didn't want to add special emphasis to it.

All of this happened when the disciples were doing their ordinary work. That's important. It's not when they are in this reflective, monastic state that all of this happens. God is showing us that he changed people who were just like you and me. You don't have to go to church to find God—he'll find you, and he'll find you in the place that you normally dwell.

Unstoppable Christian

Jesus used Peter, in part, to illustrate a concept completely foreign to Jews at the time: Grace. Peter messed up—he messed up in the worst possible way. As a good Jew, Peter felt bad, no doubt, and probably felt it was high time to get thee to the alter and sacrifice a lamb. But he was in for a surprise: a lamb couldn't save him. There were no sacrifices he himself could make. There was nothing Peter could do to be forgiven...except accept Jesus Christ and receive the grace that he freely offers.

Grace was a foreign idea to Peter. It's foreign to many of us. And it's been one of the most difficult concepts for many Christians to fully understand...which brings us to another Peter: Peter Damian.

Peter was born to a noble family about 1007; noble they were, rich they were not. Though he had a nice noble name, he did not have a nice childhood. Still he overcame, and before his 30th birthday he was already a famous teacher of theology.

While riding high in academia, he decided that this kind of lifestyle just gave him too many luxuries; he left the university where he taught and entered a life of solitude. He was essentially a hermit.

Damian, however, wasn't known for being a smart guy who became a hermit. Few would probably take note if that was the case. Damian was known for being the father of

Christian flagellation.

Flagellation, for those unfamiliar, is essentially whipping or lashing someone (including yourself). Damian came up with this idea that we could be a whole lot more devoted if we tortured ourselves. If Peter the apostle was one of his students, then grace wouldn't have brought him closer to God—a good lashing would.

Damian was devoted. Unstoppable, even. He left everything. He could have had a lavish lifestyle, but he chose instead to be a hermit. He understood grace, and yet he still felt that grace wasn't enough, that true devotion meant having to put yourself through torture. He was a wise man, and yet his wisdom could not bring him to see that no lashing could bring him closer to God. You cannot control sin with a whip. Prayer, yes. Meditation, yes. Learning, even. But if you are trying to become better through a beating, then you probably took one too many beatings to the head because it's not going to happen.

SIX

....

WHAT'S SO GREAT ABOUT A COMMISSION

Y ou've seen the opening acts, now it's time to get to the main attraction. Because when it comes down to it, the Resurrection wasn't about doing a flashy miracle; it wasn't about proving Jesus Christ was Messiah; and it wasn't to convince people to believe. It certainly did all of these things. But the Resurrection was really about Jesus giving his final teaching before assuming his place in Heaven.

The most detailed account of the Great Commission is in Matthew. In fact, aside from giving an account of the Resurrection, this is the only post-Resurrection event Matthew records. For his Gospel—for the people he was witnessing to—what transpired at the Great Commission was the single most important lesson for them to understand.

Matthew 28:16 tells us the 11 made their way to Galilee; the Bible doesn't reveal a lot about why. Did Jesus tell them in one of his appearances to get up there? Or are they finally starting to believe what Jesus told them before he died? If you need a refresher, Jesus said prior to his death that he would go to Galilee (see Matthew 26:32 and Mark 14:28). We don't even know at what mountain all of this appeared at. But none of that is important.

So, what's important? What is it that Matthew wants his reader to know? And in turn, what does Jesus want us to know? In a nutshell: that the disciples were there together. All 11 of them. Because this isn't a teaching Jesus is giving his all-star lineup—this is something they're getting as a group. That's important. The Great Commission isn't something for individual believers—it's something for all believers.

What a relief, right?! They're there together and they've finally come to terms with all of this being real! Awesome! Radical! Wrong. Because, while they did go there together, verse 17 tells us that "some doubted"! What's more, "they worshiped him; but some doubted." They worshiped him even when they doubted him! Who are these people?! Us. That's who they are.

The disciples really do represent us because that's how a lot of people would be if Jesus came today. They'd bow to the crown in worship on the outside, but still doubt on the inside. They're seeing a man come back from the dead: and they're still doubting!

It doesn't say who the "some" were, but the author wants us to know that it happened. He wants us to know that a human experience happened during a holy encounter. He wants us to know that it's ok to have doubts. The reality is, God doesn't want us to believe blindly—he wants us to look at a supernatural experience and make sure what we are seeing is of God and not of something else.

Still, Mark's account of the event (Mark 16:14-18) tells us that Jesus didn't go softly on them for their unbelief. God is patient with us, but there comes a point where we have all the evidence and we either have to take it and believe or not believe. In verse 14, it says "He rebuked them for their lack of faith and their stubborn refusal to believe those who had seen him after he had risen." (NIV)

God can use even our unbelief to his glory, because this unbelief tells us something: that there was no conspiracy. People who argue that the disciples essentially hid his body and made up a story of the Resurrection should take note here, because the Bible is essentially telling us that even the disciples—the ones who followed him and left everything for his teachings—did not expect this Resurrection and, in many ways, didn't want to even believe in it. Why conspire to do something they did not believe was possible? Had they conspired then this scene would have looked differently; the disciples wouldn't have been so confused because they expected everything—they were the ones writing the history. But that wasn't the case.

Unlike the other teachings Jesus has given, this one isn't so much a teaching than a command. The disciples had probably come to expect Jesus to mysteriously show up and tell them more things to increase their faith, but he's all done with that. His time on Earth has come to an end and he's all done trying to convince them and teach them. The only teaching he gives is Matthew 28:18: "All authority in Heaven and on earth has been given to me." (NIV)

For those who say that Jesus never said he was God, they're right. He didn't say he was God...not in that exact phrasing, that is. He said it in so many other ways, however. This verse is one example. He's telling the disciples that he has complete and total authority in both Heaven and Earth. Mere men do not make this claim. He's telling his disciples that he is God and he has the authority to say what he's about to say.

And with that final teaching, he moves on and gives them a direct command:

> Therefore, go and make disciples of all nations, baptizing them in the name of the Father and of the Son and of the Holy Spirit, and teaching them to obey everything I have commanded you. And surely, I am with you always, to the very end of the age." (Matthew 28:19-20, NIV)

This verse is weighted! First, "Therefore, go and make disciples of all nations." Some translations, such as the KJV, say "teach all nations." Both mean the same thing, but "teach" might help make it more understandable for some, because what Jesus is saying here is that the disciples are no longer students—they are teachers. He's told them what they needed to know and now it's going to be on them to tell the world about them. And that brings us to the second important point, "nation."[40] Because Jesus is instructing them

---

[40] Or world.

not to tell Jews about him, but *everyone* about him. God has just been unleashed to the world. The first covenant was between him and his chosen people, but in his second covenant we are all his chosen people.

Mark 16:15 also gives this special emphasis to preach the Gospel to Jews and Gentiles alike when he says, "Go into all the world and preach the gospel to all creation." It may seem easy to follow today, but is it really? Because there are people who you probably hide the Gospel from—maybe because you don't think they'll care? Maybe because you are embarrassed that they know you are a believer? Or maybe because you're afraid that they'll throw insults at you or challenge your faith? God does not like excuses. He's very clear here. You should preach his Gospel everywhere and to everybody—create possibilities for sharing your belief in all that you do.

Jesus continues, "…baptizing them in the name of the Father and of the Son and of the Holy Spirit" (NIV). Baptizing is important here, but more important is that second part: "name of the Father and of the Son and of the Holy Spirit." That's obviously a reference to the Trinity, but what's more: that's the first time the Trinity is ever recorded in the Bible; prior to this, the Father, Son and Holy Spirit had all been referenced in the Bible, but never together.

To put what's going on here into a little bit more context, let's go to 1 Corinthians 10:2, Paul writes that under the Old Covenant, the Jewish people were "all baptized into Moses in the cloud and in the sea." So, what Paul is saying is when a person is baptized they are essentially adopting that person as their teacher; what Jesus is saying here—commanding here—is that this old system is gone; under the New Covenant, a person is baptized and receives God as their teacher.

But why not just say, "Baptizing in the name of God"? It proves that the union is equal—Father is not greater than Son is not greater than Spirit.

Mark 16:16 adds a bit more to baptism: condemnations. "Whoever believes and is baptized will be saved, but whoever does not believe will be condemned." (NIV)

Jesus doesn't say this as a command—to go and condemn the world. He says it as a warning. Your family members who don't believe will be condemned; so will your friends; and co-workers. Everyone. Save them!

Jesus doesn't say that people who don't believe "are condemned." He says they "will be." There's a chance to save them. He says this to put urgency on the situation. Not to wait for the right opportunity, but to make every opportunity right.

So far, Christ has said in this verse his disciples are first to go out and convert, and then they are to baptize; in the next verse, he commands them to teach: "teaching them to obey everything I have commanded you." There's a word in there you should pay close attention to: I. "Everything *I* have commanded you." Jesus is telling them, they are not the judges. They don't make the law. They don't make the teachings. They teach what he has taught.

It's easy to tell people what we believe God wants others to do—how we believe he wants them to act and command. But that's not Biblical. That's not what we are commanded to do. We are commanded only to teach what Christ has taught, which we can read in the Gospels.

Finally, Christ ends with a promise: "And surely, I am with you always, to the very end of the age." (NIV) Christ's body is leaving Earth, but his spirit will dwell on the Earth as long as there are still Christians on Earth—he is protecting us, holding us up and encouraging us, and blessing us. *But* there will come an end to this age. We can't predict when this will come, nor should we predict. Christ tells us this for the same reason he has always mentioned that we don't know when the end will come—we must seize the day while we still can.

In a nutshell, the Great Commission is Christ first asserting his power and authority over all believers; he authorizes his disciples to use this authority, and finally he gives a promise.

The Great Commission is often associated with missionaries—the people called to go out and spread the messages to the corners of the world who have never heard of Christ or who don't have the resources to be taught. It's fitting, so why not use it? But the Great Commission isn't a call for missionaries. It's a call for us. It's a call for community. It's God showing us that we are one people—one church—in Christ. So far, Christ has come to the women, to the strangers, to the disciples, to the doubters, and to the leaders—now he comes to the community of believers. His teachings are spreading larger and larger; each appearance reaches a larger group.

But Mark 16:17-18 gives us just a little bit more:

And these signs will accompany those who believe: In my name, they will drive out demons; they will speak in new tongues; they will pick up snakes with their hands; and when they drink deadly poison, it will not hurt them at all; they will place their hands on sick people, and they will get well. (NIV)

There should be a few things noted about this passage. First, Jesus does not say if these things will happen for a short time or for all time. Second, it does not say everyone will have these gifts.

But let's talk about the bigger elephant in the room. There are some wacky things going on here: snake handling! Drinking poison?! How are we supposed to read this? What is the takeaway? Should we be bringing cobra snakes to church on Sunday? Should we put poison in the communion cup and just see what happens?

Pull out your Bibles. Got them? Now go ahead and read through the entire New Testament and find all the instances of people getting bit by snakes and drinking poison. Got them all. Now, let's count them up. Feel free to use just one hand; heck go ahead and just use one finger! Because there's only one instance of it.

Acts 28:3-4 tells the story of a viper jumping out at Paul, but that Paul is not harmed by the venom.

If this is supposed to be a common thing, then it would be all over the place in the Bible. Snakes jumping up in every chapter!

What gives? Why is Jesus telling it? It's not to get people excited. It's to give them an illustration. We aren't supposed to test God by taming snakes and drinking poison. But Jesus is showing that God will do these miraculous things for his glory—that when we see them happen, we can say they are from God.[41] They will happen if it is necessary to show that God protects his people.

#   #   #

God is unleashed to the community of believers in the Great Commission—nothing can stop them from getting God's message across; God will use any means to protect his community to bring that message to the unsaved. It's fitting that this last teaching gives one of the most important lessons: we aren't in this alone. We are a body of believers.

What made the disciplines grow and become unstoppable—what makes us unstoppable as believers—is knowing that we aren't in it alone. God will never ask or expect you to do anything without the support of other Christians. It may certainly feel that way at times, but if you are ever truly alone, then you should evaluate why. We have fellowship in Christ, and we have fellowship with each other.

UNSTOPPABLE CHRISTIANS

When Jesus said we should go forth and make disciples of men (Matthew 28:19), it's easy to see it as more of the closing line to a great movie. Inspiring. But it's not based on

---

[41] So leave your snakes at home!

a real story, right? We aren't supposed to actually do that, are we? We're just supposed to be happy and be nice to people, right? Because the reality is, as Christians—as humans—it's easy to become a Christian and get...comfortable. To turn the Great Commission into the Great "Let's Do Our Best to Support Missionaries Financially...Unless That's a Burden Too...At Which Point We'll Just Say We'll Keep Them in Thoughts and Prayers."[42] If we're being honest, the Great Commission is easier to read than to actually do...unless you are Amy Carmichael.

Born in 1867, Amy suffered from neuralgia.[43] It wasn't a life-ending illness, but it was enough to get you a pass when God was handing out "Who's Going to Be a Missionary?" cards. But Amy pushed forward and accepted a call to go to Asia. While in Japan, she fell ill and was sent home, but made a detour in India. She never returned home. She stayed and served India for over 50 years without a single furlough.

At the time, India had a custom of forcing children[44] into prostitution at Hindu temples; Hindu priests would serve as pimps and collect the money. Amy created a ministry to rescue the girls.

Her illness forced her to become bedridden for the last two decades of her life, but she remained in India where she

---

[42] And *sometimes* we do keep them in our prayers.

[43] A neurological condition that makes you constantly feel achy.

[44] Notably young girls.

became an author of over a dozen books. Three years before her death in 1951, India outlawed temple prostitution.

SEVEN

....

OTHER APPEARANCES

In terms of college slackers, I was as nerdy as they come. I would often ditch classes because I was in some dusty corner of the campus library reading—everything from reference books to theses from former students. I'm not entirely sure how I passed, but that's beside the point. The point is, while I was in one of these dusty corners, I came across the Christian history section and found books I'd never heard of before: apocryphal works of the New Testament. It was enough alternative history to make Dan Brown pass out in utter joy.

There was nothing secret about any of these books. They may not have been talked about in Sunday school, but they were certainly talked about everywhere else—for hundreds of years.

It's taken six chapters to get to the epic conclusion of Jesus' final time on Earth. But before getting to the closing act, there are a few more non-Gospel events that are worth examining.

Leave on a cable history channel long enough, and you'll be bound to see more than your fair share of stories about what the church doesn't want you to know. And what is it that the church doesn't want you to know? That Jesus had a twin brother, that Jesus was married, that Jesus fought dragons, the list goes on and on.

TV shows have it right. Sort of. Because these events, and more, are things referenced in books outside the Bible. What they have wrong is that they say these books are hidden from us. They are not. The books have been known for centuries. There's nothing remotely hidden about them.

The reason they aren't in the Bible isn't because of their content. If Jesus was a dragon master, trust me, you'd know! The reason is because the works that they come from are simply too late to be considered authoritative.

Think of it like this. You're studying the history of the Revolutionary War and some guy stands up and says, "Look, there's something you don't know about the war. My family has passed down secret knowledge of this war for over 200 years, and my great, great, great, great, great grandpa said George Washington crafted a gun out of his shoe." I guess that could have happened. But you won't see that added to history books anytime soon—not because it's a strange story, but because it can't be verified.

So, what are we to do? Chalk the stories up as heresy and never speak of them again? Of course not! For two reasons. One, they might be true. Two, even if they aren't true, they surely teach us about the thought process of early Christians.

There are two stories of note that tell us something about the forty days.

#   #   #

The first is The Gospel of Hebrews. Some apocryphal works are...bizarre; others might have been included in the Bible had they actually been available. The Gospel of Hebrews belongs to that second group. The book was so well-loved that it was quoted by several early church fathers. Why wasn't it included in the Bible? One of the biggest things going against it is that only fragments exist. There's no complete work available anywhere.

The Gospel reiterates what several of the New Testament gospels say, but it has one key passage that's not: a resurrection appearance to James, the Brother of Jesus:

> And when the Lord had given the linen cloth to the servant of the priest, he went to James and appeared to him. For James had sworn that he would not eat bread from that hour in which he had drunk the cup of the Lord until he should see him risen from among them that sleep. And shortly thereafter the Lord said: Bring a table and bread! And immediately it is added: He took the bread, blessed it and broke it and gave it to James the Just and said to him: My brother, eat thy bread, for the Son of man is risen from among them that sleep.

What should we make of that? First, who is James? Was he a "brother" of Christ in the literal sense or the figurative?[45] Catholics and Orthodox Christians would agree in the figurative—Mary, according to them, was a virgin for life-er. Most Protestants, however, are a little more open to

---

[45] "Fist bumps to my homie" sense.

James as a literal brother. In the case of the family variety, it makes more sense why Jesus might appear to James—it could have merely been because he was a disciple, but it also could have been because he needed to appear to family and give closure.

Family matters aside, what insight can the encounter offer us? It gives us a slightly different take on the Upper Room; unlike the other Gospel accounts, James believes in the Resurrection before it actually happens.

Mary and the Case of Perpetual Virginity

Cover your eyes, young children, because I'm about to ask one of the most pressing early theological questions of the church—one that people still ask today: Did Mary have sex?

If you err on the side of, "Is that really a thing? I thought she married Joseph and had lots of happy children?" Then you're probably wondering what gives with that whole virgin for life thing. So...what gives?

The New Testament does, of course, talk about Jesus having brothers, but those verses could mean half-brothers or more spiritual brothers. The doctrine of perpetual virginity didn't really kick into high gear until after all the apostles had died; one of the first cases for it is in an apocryphal work known as the *Protoevangelium of James*.

If you believe in the doctrine of virgin 'til death, that's

likely based on how you view Mary. Is Mary just Mary, or to carry the child of God, doesn't she have to be holier than that? Fans of the doctrine essentially believe that Mary represented the faithful spouse to the Holy Spirit who impregnated her—having relations with her Earthly husband meant she was cheating on the Spirit. Cheating may have been the case *before* birth, but after birth the question is whether or not she was still married to the Holy Spirit in the absolute literal sense.

The Catholic and Orthodox Churches aren't without their fair argument—translators have argued with valid points both for and against the perpetual virginity. The importance of their argument can extend into another theological belief they hold as true: the assumption of Mary. Contrary to what some believe, assumption doesn't mean she was taken away before she died (though some hold that to be the case). What does it mean? Well nobody likes to be a Debbie downer, but many Christians believe we don't go to Heaven when we die—we go there when Christ returns for us. We're essentially just chilling in our graves. There's certainly room to disagree here, but, fret not, it's not like you'll be bored out of your mind in a coffin—you won't even know you've been dead. But if you believe in the assumption of Mary, then basically you believe that we die and wait, but Mary didn't have to wait—she was taken straight away to Heaven; for that to happen, however, they hold she would have had to remain pure and not have sexual relations.

While not having sex with Joseph would certainly make Mary devoted, the question you really have to ask is: does it matter?

The Gospel of Bartholomew doesn't mess around when it comes to the Resurrection; unlike the Gospels, which spend pretty much the entire account talking about Jesus' teaching, Bartholomew gets right to the Resurrection—and then he gets to hell.

In his account,[46] Jesus is almost like an action hero—he's on a mission from God, he's in hell, and it's payback time. It has all the makings of an epic—angels, torture, and, of course, Bible heroes like Adam.

What the account doesn't have is much truth. The theme of predestination is a big one in the book.

Jesus goes to hell again in another apocryphal work, the Gospel of Nicodemus—this time he even manhandles Satan and turns him over to be tortured. The account, like that of Bartholomew, is hundreds of years after the fact. Both of these stories have been deemed Gnostic accounts.

What's a Gnostic you may ask?

Luke 1:1 gives us our first clues about this wacky thing known as Gnosticism. He writes, "Many have undertaken to

---

[46] And by his, I mean some other guy because this was certainly not written by Bartholomew, the apostle—it was written hundreds of years after.

draw up an account of the things that have been fulfilled among us." (NIV) Luke could be referencing other Gospel writers, but the word "many" might also mean more people than just the Gospel writers have taken to writing accounts; and the fact that he's careful to point out that his will be more historical implies the others maybe have been not so truthful.

That's a lot of maybes. Let's get to the certainties of the Gnostics.

Gnostics believed they possessed a secret knowledge of God. They would make up outlandishly bizarre stories and say it was true because God told it just to them. Mormons could certainly fall into this territory, because their entire religion is based on an account of a man who had a secret revelation from God.

Luke's Gnostics were probably not quite as crazy; they were likely just people who got bad accounts of a story. The wackier Gnostics started popping up in the second and third centuries. By this time all the eyewitnesses of Jesus had died and it made it easier for a person to pop up and make stuff up. If a person claimed to have secret knowledge earlier than this, an eyewitness could just stand up and say, "This dude is out of his mind. We were there. This definitely didn't happen." And that was that.

\#   \#   \#

There is one final account—albeit a Biblical one—that tells us what went on during these forty days.

In 1 Corinthians 15:6, Paul gives us a tidbit not included anywhere else in the Bible: "After that, he appeared to more than five hundred of the brothers and sisters at the same time, most of whom are still living, though some have fallen asleep." (NIV)

500! Wow! Awesome, right?! Except, doesn't Acts 1:15 say Christ appeared to 120?

Did Paul just give the gotcha moment that skeptics would swoop up and use against Christians? Sort of. Because skeptics do in fact use this as a way of saying the Bible contradicts itself.

Before you run off and join the skeptic brigade, pause for a moment and consider what's happening here.

First, there's a word in the Corinthians verse that skeptics don't like: "eita."

Like a lot of words in the Bible, there's a lot of room for interpretation when it comes to translation. The original Greek uses the word "eita" in the verse, which means "afterward" or "furthermore." So, while the quick glance reading will tell you Paul is giving a sequence of events—a timeframe of when things happened, if you will; what Paul is really giving is a sequence of eyewitness accounts that he felt important. He's not saying, "This happened and *then* this and *then* this." He's saying, "This happened and this happened and this happened."

Most scholars believe Corinthians was written before the Acts of the Apostle; so, Luke, who wrote Acts, would have likely known all about Paul and that 500 number—he was, after all, interviewing witnesses. It seems reasonable that Luke would have come just a tad bit closer to that number if they are talking about the same events.

If that 500 number isn't just Paul giving the wrong number for what should be 120, then what is the 500?

There are different ways to look at it. First you could say Luke isn't counting a lot of things into that 120 number—like women; or that there were 500 there but only 120 were what Luke would define as disciples.

But the more logical way would be that this 500 was an appearance prior to the 120 that simply is not recorded anywhere else. In Matthew 28:10 Jesus says, "Go and tell my brothers to go to Galilee; there they will see me." (NIV) Many suspect that this is when the appearance happened, but the time and place of the event really isn't important. In fact, many early church fathers believed that it happened a year after the Resurrection. It's the event that's important.

As has been said already, each New Testament writer had different audiences that they were writing to. Paul isn't writing a book to convert people like the Gospel writers were. He's writing to people who are believers, but are having a dispute within the church.

Paul writes that Jesus appeared to Peter, the 12, the 500, and to himself as well. What's he telling the church in the letter? He's giving a list of eyewitnesses who have authority over the church. He's telling them that they have people they can go to—that it isn't just these 12 little guys that they have to believe; there are literally hundreds who can give testament of the events. He's telling them that they can't just go about and make up their own gospel—nor should they have to, because there's plenty of facts out there that tell them exactly what they need to know.

Jesus Ascended. What Does That Mean?

We don't, unfortunately, know what happened when Jesus appeared to the 500; one can only imagine it was some teaching. But Paul wants his readers to know it. And God wants us to know it. Why? Because it helps cement the fact that these events happened. Jesus didn't appear to a handful. He appeared to over 500 at one time! It's easy to say Mary(s) were in shock and just saw what they thought was Jesus; that the disciples stole the body; that the two men walking that Jesus appeared to were simply nuts; that Paul had a seizure and saw some wacky vision; that...it's easy to keep making excuses.

500 is no longer an intimate encounter; it's a concert! It's a gathering.

God appeared to 500 because that's what he felt people needed. 500 people witnessed this. If you are going to deny it and believe that more than 500 were crazy, fine. Because if you can't believe in 500, then you won't believe in 1,000 or 10,000. God gives us enough—faith gives us the rest. You either have to submit to faith—submit to God—or just walk away because nothing is going to make you believe.

God is selective. He reveals not what we want to know, but what we need to know. That's how we should approach the forty days. We should look at what he shows us and ask, "What does God want us to know?"

Once you consider that, then you can move on to the Ascension.

UNSTOPPABLE CHRISTIAN

Some of the New Testament apocrypha was downright wacky tabacky; but every once in a while, there were stories of Christians who were unstoppable. Perpetua's life wasn't just unstoppable—it was legendary. So, legendary, in fact, that Augustine once warned Christians against making her story equal to the Bible.

Perpetua was born in the second century to a wealthy, but pagan, family; around 201 AD, when the emperor of Rome forbade conversions to Christianity. Perpetua and many others were among those rounded up. She was a brand-new Christian who was preparing to be baptized.

So, off she goes to prison, where things aren't as bad as they could have been—they let her dear old dad visit to try and convince her to renounce her faith, and even allow her to breastfeed her newly born child. When she refused to renounce her faith, she was sentenced to death in the arena.

According to legend,[47] she kept a diary of her life in prison leading up to her death and sneaked it off to another person. It became the *Diary of Anne Frank* of her day, and was read in churches for hundreds of years.

---

[47] And by legend, I mean some have argued some of this.

EIGHT

....

THE ASCENSION

A nd now we at last arrive. The moment we've all been waiting for: The Ascension.

The greatest post-Resurrection miracle is, of course, the Ascension. But why? Why was it so important for Jesus to ascend into Heaven? What happened when it happened, and what happened because it happened? Does it even matter to us today? Did it *really* matter to the disciples back then?

Let's rewind a little bit before going forward. Why did the disciples need to be at the Ascension? They weren't at his Resurrection. Why is this encounter so special? In a word: Proof.

The proof of the Resurrection is that Jesus Christ stood in front of them. Of course, he resurrected! You don't have to see the moment of resurrection to know he has been raised. But how do you prove the Ascension? They needed to be there. They needed to be eyewitnesses to the event.

But why Ascension at all?

Ephesians 4:8 tells us when Christ ascended, he led "captivity captive" (KJV)—in other words he conquered sin and death; this itself is something that Psalm 68:18 predicted;[48] in his death on the cross, Christ was sacrificing himself for all mankind. Prior to this, Jews had to offer a sacrifice for the forgiveness of sin; Christ put an end to that. But through his Resurrection and Ascension, he proved that he not only defeated sin, but he also defeated death.

Jesus promised his disciples that he would leave this Earthly world, but that he will "give you another advocate to help you and be with you forever." (John 14:16, NIV) Jesus ascends to Heaven with the promise of the Holy Spirit.

The Ascension also fulfills the promise that Jesus will return to the Father. John 16:28: "I came from the Father and entered the world; now I am leaving the world and going back to the Father."

Finally, Jesus is ascending to create a place for us. John 14:2 "if that were not so, would I have told you that I am going there to prepare a place for you?"

The Ascension meant many other things, of course. It was the symbolic conclusion of his ministry on Earth. It showed a visual path of his return to Heaven—the disciples would be able to confidently say that Christ not only rose from the dead, but that he dwells in Heaven. It marks the beginning of a new age—Heaven opened up and will reopen when he returns to Earth.

---

[48] "You have ascended on high, you have led captivity captive." (NIV)

Jewish Sacrifice

Jews no longer make alter sacrifices because their temple was destroyed in 70 AD; the numerologist fan inside me will point out that Jesus died in either 30 AD or 33 AD; scholars have argued both dates, but if we date his death at 30 AD and the temple was destroyed in 70 AD, then that's a forty year gap—forty day gap between the Resurrection and Ascension; forty year gap between the Resurrection and complete end of temple sacrifice.

But what's the deal with sacrifice anyway? If you need a quick refresher, when God established a covenant with the people of Israel; Jews would offer a sacrifice—sometimes, but not always, an animal—as atonement for sin. Christians believe Jesus established a new covenant not with one people, but all people, and he is the atonement for our sins.

If Jews no longer have a temple to make sacrifices in and they don't believe Christ can give them forgiveness, then how do they believe they are forgiven? The main way is Tzedakah. Tzedakah is the act of giving to those in need. Orthodox Jews still believe the temple will be rebuilt and sacrifices will resume.

#   #   #

If you knew you were going to die—be taken up to Heaven—what would your last words be? Your family is all gathered around you, anticipating what you might say. This is their last memory of you on Earth.

The composer Beethoven went with simple for his last words, "Friends applaud, the comedy is finished." Emily Dickinson went with a poetic, "I must go in, the fog is rising." And American frontiersman Kit Carson went with chili, "I just wish I had time for one more bowl of chili."[49]

It's with this last moment—the last words of Jesus Christ before leaving Earth—that Luke has left us. Jesus knows his forty days are up. It's time to ascend into Heaven. It's time to leave his followers with parting words. But we don't get to hear them. All this buildup and we don't even know what he said?! Sort of. Because while we don't know what he said, we know what he did. Luke says he, "lifted up his hands and blessed them."[50]

His final act on Earth was a blessing.

Stop and think about that for a second. Most people just want to get in one last word—one wise thing to be remembered by. There were words here, for sure; Mark 16:19 says, "After the Lord Jesus had spoken to them," (NIV) which clearly shows there were words. But it's the action that is remembered. In his last act, he made it about them.

What else do we know? His hands are risen. Okay. Who cares, right? But why are they risen? Two things come to mind. One, he is showing authority. But two, and perhaps more importantly, he is separated from them. When you

---

[49] He must have really loved chili.

[50] Luke 24:50

think of a blessing, what do you think about? Normally it's someone laying a hand over someone. Not so here, however. It's as if Christ is laying his hands over the entire world— not just a group of people—the blessing is radiating out— not onto specific people, but out onto the world.

The Ascension itself is pretty darn incredible. But it's not unique. Elijah ascended to Heaven. 2 Kings 2:11 says, "As they were walking along and talking together, suddenly a chariot of fire and horses of fire appeared and separated the two of them, and Elijah went up to Heaven in a whirlwind." (NIV) But this Ascension is different. Elijah needed angels. Christ went to Heaven by his own power.

Finally, both Luke and Mark tell us he didn't ascend any old place; he ascended into Heaven. Heaven is obviously important because…well, it's Heaven! But it's more than that. On Earth, he was limited by space and time. Heaven defies all the rules of Earth. Jesus is no longer bound in one physical place. He is now boundless—he can travel every- where and to anybody—fully accessible all the time.

#   #   #

When you think of the Ascension, you might have a pic- ture in your head. If you're like a lot of people, maybe it's grandiose: fireworks in the sky, flames shooting from Jesus' eyeballs, a mariachi band randomly playing in the back- ground, because, why not? It's very human to think this way. Because when we think "God" the only thing we can think is something powerful—like Thor. But God sees larger than life differently. I'm sure God knows all about Thor, but his conception of mighty and epic is much different than yours and mine. When you think about the Ascension, try your best to get out of human mindset.

It's impossible to paint a picture of the Ascension because we weren't there and there's no accounts from eyewitnesses that describe it in detail. So, we have to guess. I imagine it wasn't as epic as my imagination might assume. It was probably simple and beautiful—a piece of the sky opening and just a tiny fragment of Heaven being revealed.

In some ways, it's interesting that he ascended at all; Heaven, after all, isn't in the sky. If you float high enough, you don't reach it. Jesus could have just as easily walked into Heaven, I suppose. But God is giving the disciples the best representation of Heaven that they knew. To these men, Heaven probably was in the sky.

The details really don't matter. The ministry matters. What follows matters.

Some have concluded that the Ascension was in fact a spiritual act—that he didn't actually ascend in the physical sense of the word. But that doesn't make sense. Think about it like this: you're at an important meeting; it's one of those meetings that can make or break you. You're just about to go in and your phone vibrates: a text from your partner, who's making the presentation with you; it reads, "I'm sorry, but I can't make it—but I'll be with you in spirit." How do you think that meeting is going to go? Do you think your partner will be with you in spirit? No! Being there in spirit does nothing for you! Maybe you do okay on the presentation, but what's going to happen when you see your partner?

Are you going to high five him and say, "I couldn't have did it if you weren't there with me in spirit." Absolutely not!

If Jesus had merely "spiritually" ascended, then the change that happens next to the disciples would not have happened. They saw something—they saw the physical Ascension of Jesus Christ. That's what motivated the ministry that was about to follow them for the rest of their days on Earth.

#　　#　　#

After the Ascension, the disciples seem instantly changed. They still haven't received the promised Holy Spirit.[51] But it says in Luke 24:52 that they worshiped him. No longer is Jesus the teacher or the prophet—this is a different kind of worship. This is the worship you give to God and to God alone.

What must be remembered about what happened next is there's a gap. Acts continues where Luke let off, but the Holy Spirit doesn't come after the Ascension—not right after, anyway. The disciples return to Jerusalem with the expectation of what's to come—the promise of an advocate. And so, it's hard not to wonder what that waiting period was like. They probably stayed near the temple worshiping God in preparation. We know how many days they waited,[52] but they did not.

The experience is something most of us sadly don't know. Worship for most of us is the singing we do on Sun-

---

[51] Spoiler alert, that's the next chapter.

[52] FYI, 10.

days. These guys were putting this kind of worship to shame.

I'm not sure I can fully imagine this kind of worship, but I don't imagine something that was charismatic—disciples dancing and singing in the streets. I think they gathered in close communion, and they prayed. I imagine it was a very intimate time as God prepared their hearts and they listened. There was probably more silence than talking—meditating on what would happen next.

When we think about Peter and John and the other all-star disciple lineup, we think of strong, courageous men; but I don't think this was the case—at least here. I think there was still a lot of fear and confusion. The disciples weren't that different than you and me—they had the greatest teacher who ever lived, but they were still men. God chose them because they were like you and me. As they worshiped, they probably were talking amongst each other about what this meant.

I used to think, if I prayed hard enough, then I could be this radical Christian—that I could go out there and speak to anyone and instantly convert them. I used to think that. God doesn't make radical Christians overnight—He makes them over time. If God were to radicalize a person, then it wouldn't be authentic—it would be forced. And God's not into forcing people into doing things. What God does instead is, He lets us change at the pace that we believe—radicalize as truth is revealed.

That's what's happening as they worship God here. He's slowly preparing them for what's going to happen next.

Jesus Ascended. What Does That Mean?

#   #   #

Jesus' death was really a seed in the ground; he died so his seed could be planted and it could rise to produce fruit.

Mark ends a little differently than Luke—not contradictory—just different. Mark 16:20 says, "Then the disciples went out and preached everywhere, and the Lord worked with them and confirmed his word by the signs that accompanied it." (NIV)

We aren't supposed to go out into the world and say that Christ rose. We're supposed to go out and prove it—show God manifested in the works and actions that we do.

Maybe you're a great debater, and you can win a person to Christianity with your words. But rarely do conversions happen during debates. They happen over actions. They happen when people look at you and say, "Something is different about that person—I want to be like that."

You can't see Christ in words—you can only hear his name and hear his deeds. But you can see Christ in love; you can see him when there's a person who is acting out of love—doing something completely out of their character.

The world doesn't need radical words—it needs radical actions. That's what's about to happen with the disciples. The world is about to see men and women go out into the world and show we are all equal—there is neither Jew nor Gentile; male or female. In Christ, we are one creation. The theology will blow people away because it's the first time they're seeing something that unites instead of divides people. It's not a message for the Jews or for the rich or the poor—it's a message for all mankind. It's a message that isn't inward but rather outward—not about finding yourself, but helping others.

In love—in their actions, not their words—they are able to prove that Christ is real.

UNSTOPPABLE CHRISTIAN

The Ascension is Christ going to Heaven and paying for our salvation. We were spiritual slaves and he saved us—he bought our freedom out of this spiritual slavery. Millions of Christians, while spiritually free, were physically chained. Amanda Smith was part of the physically chained group…but she didn't let those chains stop her from moving the kingdom of Christ forward.

Amanda Smith was born in 1837; as a child, her father would perform his daily duties as a slave, and then spend the night (sometimes not sleeping) working more hours to earn enough money to buy his family's freedom. Like pretty much every African American of her day, she had it tough, but you could easily say she had it even tougher than most— by the age of 32, she had lost two husbands and four children. To work through her grief, she became active in the African Methodist Episcopal Church.

There were plenty of good 'ol white people preaching the Gospel. But African Americans? Not so much. Smith did what few African Americans before her (and a woman on top of that) did—she went to churches and spoke in front of audiences of hundreds about Jesus Christ. It was new and even unheard of.

By the time of her death, she had opened an orphanage, traveled and preached around the world, and written a book: *An Autobiography, The Story of the Lord's Dealing with Mrs. Amanda Smith, the Colored Evangelist Containing an Account of her Life Work of Faith, and Her Travels in America, England, Ireland, Scotland, India, and Africa, as An Independent Missionary.*[53]

---

[53] The title kind of gives the entire plot away, but if you'd like to read it, it's in public domain, which means you can download it for free.

NINE

....

PENTECOST

I spent my childhood in school. When I graduated, I went straight to college and was back in school. When I finished that, I went to grad school where—you guessed it—I was in school.

When I finished grad school, it was eye-opening. In some ways, I wasn't prepared. I didn't know anything but school. That's kind of where the disciples are—it's been all Jesus all the time; and now that phase is over, and their next chapter is beginning. It's a scary time, but God's going to get them through it. In many ways, it's what we experience in our own life—we accept Christ and we feel instantly changed...but that's really just the beginning for us: the real fireworks begin when we start to learn what it *really* means to accept Christ.

Fifty days have now passed since the Ascension. But if you thought the Ascension was it, then you're in for a shocker, because God has yet to give his encore performance: The Pentecost.

Jesus Ascended. What Does That Mean?

The Ascension was Jesus ascending into Heaven; Pentecost is The Spirit descending to Earth. It ties everything together. God spent forty days teaching his disciples; he's going to spend the next few seconds unleashing himself to the world. The disciples are about to learn what it *really* means to accept Christ, and the fire that starts here will never be put out.

#   #   #

Easter's fun. Who doesn't like bunnies hiding eggs from kids?[54] But if you really want to celebrate something, then Pentecost might make a better case for important holiday—in terms of what happened, you might even say Pentecost is the most important holiday of all Christianity. And yet, we're lucky if we get even a single sermon on it once a year. In fact, for the majority of churchgoing Christians, Pentecost represents that time of year when the pastor says, "Hey everyone! Did you know it's Pentecost today?!" And then the pastor goes on to preach something entirely different. That's a shame.

Before we consider why this event is so important, let's think about why it happened when it did. Why not three days after the Ascension? Or 12? Those are good Biblical numbers! Heck, why not even make it happen during the Ascension itself? God's already busy opening and closing the doors of Heaven—why not just make it easy on himself and get in a two for one deal?

---

[54] It turns out, lots of people.

God can tell us for sure why he does what he does one day, but we can no doubt turn to the date and see the symbols. Namely, that this day is a holiday.

Christians have Christmas; Jews have Passover. This is one of the most important holidays for any Jew. It represents the new covenant they have with God. Pentecost is known to Jews as Shavuot; it marks the end of Passover. Some Jews traditionally hold that Shavuot is also the day that King David was born (and died).[55]

If you think that the believers just happened to be hanging out at the right place and the right time and this whole Shavuot thing is merely coincidental, then you're obviously mistaken. We may call Christians, Christian—but 2,000 years ago, Christians were Jews. They just happened to be Jews who believed that Jesus was the fulfillment of prophecy. But they still practiced things as any good Jew would. And that meant Shavuot.

Jesus said to wait when he left them. And this is the moment he told them to wait for. So, it shouldn't seem all too coincidental that God chose the day that marked the end of a festival celebrating the most sacred Old Testament covenant to mark the start of a new covenant—one not exclusive to Judaism, but open to all believers.

So, here they all are, sitting together, getting their Shavuot on, when in came "a sound from Heaven as of a rushing mighty wind." (Acts 2:2, NIV) Think about this room.

---

[55] So, strap yourselves in, fans of "Chase's Calendar of Events"—this day's a big one.

Jesus Ascended. What Does That Mean?

This is the Upper Room that they were in with Jesus during the Last Super. It's probably not a large room and these sounds were probably bouncing all over the room. We may read this and think, "Awe! Beautiful!" But the reality is, they were probably peeing their pants right about now. They have seen literally just about every miracle you can think of, and now this! This mighty, powerful, forceful sound crashing into the room. I can imagine all of them were at least thinking, "Now what?!"

But this whole depiction is also very descriptive. You can make things up. You can exaggerate. But this description is so detailed, it seems as if it could only have come from eyewitness accounts, and that's because it did come from eyewitness accounts.

The verse continues that this Spirit "filled the whole house." This Spirit is all-encompassing—a reoccurring theme we will now see in the New Testament. The Spirit doesn't just fill people—it fills places.

And when the sounds had filled the place, the tongues of fire came out (Verse 3); it's an odd image until you think about what fire represents; it's preparing these men and women's hearts for being filled with the Spirit of God. It's burning their hearts—melting their pride, their sin—melting all that they were—so the Spirit can dwell inside of them. The spirit doesn't dwell in the heart of a sinful man—you can't say "Spirit fill me" while you're robbing a liquor store or spewing hate at a person,[56] because your heart needs to be in the right place to receive it.

Once the Spirit encompasses them, something beautiful happens; Acts 2:4 says, "All of them were filled with the Holy Spirit and began to speak in other tongues as the Spirit enabled them." It's unfortunate, but the hero of this verse for many people is they spoke in tongues. Tongues can sometimes feel like the black sheep of Christianity. It's the thing that crazy Christians do. What should not be overlooked is what happens before the tongues, "they were filled with the Holy Spirit." The thing that Christ tells them to wait for has come: the very presence of God now dwells inside of them. And it dwells inside every person that believes. It's not a Peter thing. Or a John thing. Or even a disciple thing. The Spirit is with every single person and it's with them in the same exact manner. No person is greater.

God is with all of us. He's with Muslims. He's with atheists. He's with all people equally. But it's only Christians whom God dwells in—whose very Spirit is alive in them. It's not a Spirit who meets your body at the door on Sunday morning. Or a Spirit who welcomes you when you get bad news, but that you hang at the door when you go out to party. It's a Spirit that never leaves you. That's always with you.

#   #   #

---

[56] Well you can, but it's kind of pointless.

Does Everyone Who Has a Tongue, Speak in Tongues?

What's the deal with tongues? The action sure sounds Biblical, and yet step into the wrong church today and the act of tongues can seem almost...comical. Is this like *really* a thing you're supposed to believe in? Sort of. But it depends on who you ask.

If you want to get all technical about it, then start by not referring to it as "speaking in tongues"; the clinical word is: glossolalia.[57]

Glossolalia was a thing. The Spirit has its own language, and these apostles were speaking it. But here's where it gets sticky: does it happen today?

There are certainly those who feel that it does.

But what if you aren't one of them? Well, there's evidence that it doesn't as well. One perfectly accepted theological belief is that the Gift of the Spirit was something that happened in the early church; God used to communicate his covenant with believers of the early church—to essentially give them the power to write a New Testament canon of works that was God's breath. After that was complete, there was no need to continue to give the gift to believers.

---

[57] Which, in fairness, sounds an awful lot like something you have a few hours after eating a Doritos® Cheesy Gordita Crunch taco with "beef" from *Taco Bell.*

There are also those who believe it still can happen, and sometimes does, but it's not a regular occurrence.

Regardless of what you believe, speaking in tongues is not to be taken lightly. One of the reasons the early church got in trouble was Gnostics who tried to make up their secret teachings based on what the Spirit told them. You must prayerfully consider whether or not what you are perceiving as the Spirit is actually just a crazy person mimicking a fake language.

Onlookers are baffled by the events happening; some rationalize it in verse 13 by saying they are only drunk. But verse 6 says something interesting, "Each one heard their own language being spoken." (NIV) This might bring back fond memories of the Tower of Babel for fans of the Old Testament.

The Tower of Babel represents separation. One language, scattered. And right after this story, we hear about Abraham—the man who essentially started Judaism.

So, what's happening here? God separated the world with Judaism, but here God is returning the unity that it once had with Christianity.

Many people heard what was happening, and no doubt believed as a result. The fact that some people just passed it off as a bunch of drunks is not surprising. Some people have hardened hearts. A miracle happens in front of them and they still make excuses.

Jesus Ascended. What Does That Mean?

# # #

Peter takes the stage in verse 14, and he's a changed man. He's taken his place as a leader in the church and believers are turning to him to understand what happens next. He's transformed from fisher of fish to fisher of men.

He's face-to-face with Jews who believe they're all crazy, and he's now going to make his case. It doesn't give an account of who these Jews are, but it's not hard to imagine that these are the very Jews who persecuted Jesus. These are the people who shouted "crucify him" less than two months ago. These are the people who are probably looking for an excuse to kill Peter himself. Verse 14 says that Peter "raised his voice"—he was a man of confidence. The man who had betrayed Jesus to save his life is now speaking up boldly as if his own life doesn't matter.[58]

He's not only speaking boldly, he's speaking Biblically. He's speaking Joel. Good little Jewish boys obviously knew their Hebrew. But this is Peter—a fisherman. This isn't a theologian. This is a guy who caught fish for a living. And he has found the perfect verse to explain the fulfillment of prophecy that is happening.

His sermon isn't exactly roses and buttercups. It's harsh. He tells them the facts in verse 22-24—a man came and did miraculous things...and you killed him. Enter in the big gulp. But Peter isn't finished with his sermon. Because the

---

[58] He finally understands what it means to die to self and live for Christ.

man they handed over to death could not be killed—he could not be stopped.

That certainly got their attention! By verse 37, they asked, "Brothers, what shall we do?" (NIV); old Peter probably would have said, "Bend down your necks, that we may cut them off and you can spend all of your days being tortured for your actions." But this is not old Peter—this is the Peter filled with the Spirit. His reply isn't vengeful. It's forgiving, "Repent and be baptized" he tells them in verse 38, "And you will receive the gift of the Holy Spirit." (NIV)

3,000 people became Christians that day according to verse 41. Talk about a powerful sermon! But the details of that number are sketchy at best. 3,000 people would not have fit in that Upper Room. So, what exactly happened? Did Peter go out to a bigger space and preach?

Guesswork is required here. But to begin with, it seems essential to understand that Peter isn't the only Christian here. He may have given the sermon, but there are other ministers present. What is perhaps more believable is that after the Holy Spirit came upon them, a great commotion was caused and people came toward the Upper Room to see what was happening. Think about an accident on the freeway—one accident, thousands of people slowing down to look.

What's probably happened is thousands of people are trying to figure out what all this commotion is about, and the believers leave the Upper Room, and they go tell them. There are 120 in the Upper Room; divide that by 3,000 and you get 25. That means statistically, these 120 people filled with the very Spirit of God only need to find 25 people to tell them about Jesus. If that happens, you get 3,000. That seems like a very believable number.

# # #

Pentecost is an important event. It represents two things for every Christian:

The day a new covenant essentially comes to town and gives birth to Christianity.

The day God reveals himself in the most personal way: The Holy Spirit. It marks the beginning of when all men and women cannot just know of God, but experience God.

The Resurrection was just the event that planted a seed for change for the believers—God spent 50 days growing that seed until it all culminated here. And now it's time for these men and women to go fearlessly to all the world, spreading the Good News.

UNSTOPPABLE CHURCH

The church is only as unstoppable as the Christians inside of it. But churches, no doubt, do play a role in the spread of Christianity. The 1801 Cane Ridge Revival at the Cane Ridge Meeting House is often cited as the birth of the second great awakening.

Cane Ridge is a small town about 20 miles outside of Lexington. Low estimates say 10,000 people attended the meetings; high estimates say 30,000 people. The population of the entire state for Kentucky was about 220,000 at the time. Which means at least 5% of the entire state was at the meeting, but it was probably closer to 10%. Pretty big, right? And remember, this is 1800—cars had not been invented. To get to this event was an all-day affair. And people didn't go home. They camped out. For the 1800s, this was probably the closest thing to the modern-day Coachella Music Festival.

The meetinghouse obviously wouldn't hold all of the people. So, pastors made the best of what they had. There were several stages and several pastors speaking at the same time. It was wild. Pastors standing on tree stumps, covered wagons—whatever they could find.

Part of the success could be attributed to Christians of all backgrounds coming together. This wasn't a Baptist affair. All denominations got involved. Presbyterian, Methodist and Baptist ministers all took turns delivering sermons.

While we don't really know what happened on Pentecost in that Upper Room, it's easy to imagine it looked a little something like this revival—perhaps a little small at first, but then larger and larger until it was spilling out everywhere and Christians were using whatever they could find to preach the Gospel to all who would hear.

....

EPILOGUE

S omething happened.

Something indeed. The disciples had discovered what Jesus Christ had spent his entire ministry getting them ready for. They went from seeing the human side of Christ to the godly side.

Suddenly, the man they followed was more than a man—but it wasn't the Resurrection alone that proved this; throughout the small fragments that exists in each of the Gospels and Acts are small revelations and clues about the divine nature of Christ and his relationship with us. For forty days, Christ taught his disciples what it meant to have a relationship with God; finally, at Pentecost, we see transformed men and women who finally understand what it means to have a personal relationship with God.

Easter is an important day for Christians. It represents an important event. Jesus Christ rose from the dead—he became the sacrificial lamb for our sins.

But next time you celebrate Easter, ask yourself this: what if that was it? What if Easter happened, and Jesus rose from the dead, but there was no Ascension. Jesus went on living—teaching; maybe in forty more years he died of natural causes. What then?

What is Easter—what is Christianity—without the Ascension? It's just a nice story, really. It's the story of Lazarus. A man who rose from the dead. I bet Lazarus led a full life after that—he witnessed to people and said what an amazing thing God had done. And that would have been Jesus. Because the Resurrection is just a miracle when you take the Ascension out of the equation.

If Jesus Christ had merely risen from the dead, then he would be of Earth. Fully man. He didn't Ascend to Heaven because…why not? There was a purpose there. He assumed his role in Heaven for us. Hebrews 9:24 says, "For Christ did not enter a sanctuary made with human hands that was only a copy of the true one; he entered Heaven itself, now to appear for us in God's presence." (NIV) What does this mean? It means Christ didn't conquer the temple on Earth— he didn't assume his place as a priest who was human. He ascended into Heaven—a task a mere human cannot do— and he intercedes for us.

If Jesus Christ had merely resurrected, then we could not have a personal relationship with God. Man would stand on Earth; God would stand in Heaven. But no bridge would connect us to God. Christ is that bridge—his Ascension, not his Resurrection, represented that.

But the Ascension isn't just for us. Ephesians 4:10 says, "He who descended is the very one who ascended higher than all the Heavens, in order to fill the whole universe." (NIV) Notice the word "universe" there? Is this the makings of something that's out of this world? The Jesus of aliens we don't even know? Perhaps. But more than that, it represents mankind in the most all-encompassing sense. If Jesus had not ascended, then his Resurrection would have been for the age—not the ages. It would have been a great event—a memorable event, indeed—but he would have stayed on Earth. His Ascension represents something out of this world—something with no beginning and no end. Something that doesn't care for the men and women from two thousand years ago, but cares for the people not even born—the people two thousand years in the present—or even two hundred million years in the present. All men. For all time.

For forty days, Jesus was teaching his disciples about this new body—this is new teaching. Prior to the Resurrection, his teachings were about others. But now there's a special emphasis on relationships. On how God dwells in us forever. The disciples began to change when they saw how this worked—when they saw how the Holy Spirit worked—when they saw how it all came together perfectly.

Ephesians 5:30 says, "For we are members of his body, of his flesh, and of his bones." (NIV) That's what he spent forty days teaching. It's about dying to self. Becoming part of Christ. When you no longer live, but Christ lives in you, what does that mean? Suddenly our daily worries no longer exist. We don't wake up in the morning and worry about how we'll pay the bills or how we'll feel happier. We live to show Christ to the world. That's all that matters. Yes, you still have to pay the bills and yes you still have to live in this world, but you do so with the assurance that God will provide. That he will not leave you.

But Ephesians 5:30 is more than that. Because we are "members" of his body. *Members*. That means it's not just you and him. It means we're in this together. We are a community of believers living with one common goal.

The Ascension also represents unity—Christ leaving us to join us together.

Peter may have been the hero at Pentecost—the voice of the body. But the voice is not the most important part of the church. No part is the most important, except the center, which is Christ.

The Gospel didn't spread—Christianity didn't grow— because we had people like Peter or even Paul evangelizing. One man can start a movement, but a group of men can change the world. And so, when Christ ascended into Heaven, he was uniting us. He was making us members of one body.

Christianity was a very small sect of Judaism before the Ascension. Jesus didn't leave the world with a huge following, but he did leave the world with small following who could make his name—his kingdom—huge.

The disciples—the early men—were by no means perfect. We have scandals now and they surely had them then.

But when they let the Holy Spirit dwell in them...the things that would happen!

It's easy to believe in the holidays. Christmas. Easter. And everything in between. But the holidays aren't the events that shaped Christianity—that shape us as believers. They get people to come out once or twice a year to sit in a pew and spew out a few festive tunes to make mom happy. But that's not Christianity. Christianity is in the events like the Ascension, which we don't even think about—the events that, when you are open to it, will change your heart and start a revolution inside of you.

#   #   #

When people think of being a Christian, they often think of people going to church; but Christ didn't return here to tell people about church—in fact, church was never part of Christ's message on Earth. Making disciples was his message. We aren't put on Earth to go to church on Sundays. That's not to say we should use that as an excuse not to go—but that is to say some Christians need to reevaluate their purpose in life.

Luke 14:4 tells the parable of the lost sheep:

> Suppose one of you has a hundred sheep and loses one of them. Doesn't he leave the ninety-nine in the open country and go after the lost sheep until he finds it? (NIV)

The church is fine. It's survived for thousands of years without your help. But there are lost sheep. The Ascension is about finding them.

The disciples realized there was something better—even more miraculous than the Resurrection. They realized that we can have a personal relationship with God, and further that we can give others this relationship. Jesus Christ returned not to show the world a miracle, but to show the world love.

We should think about the church; we should think about the ministries to build people up; we should think about how we can have a better relationship with God. But before we think about any of that, we must remember Christ's command to make disciples—that should be the forefront mission of every Christian.

Not all of us are ministers. Not all of us are even great speakers. But the message of Christianity is simple: God loves us unconditionally—and he forgives us. You don't need to be a minister or great speaker to show that. The 12 disciples that Jesus called to spread his message weren't educated men; most of them weren't the types you'd see at universities or writing books; but they accepted his call and God used them.

Whoever you are and whatever you do, God has called you and he can use you for his purpose. He uses the weak just as he uses the strong. He has given you a command to make disciples.

UNSTOPPABLE CHRISTIANS

There may be a lot of things holding you back—keeping you from being unstoppable. For many, it's age. Your younger years have passed you, so how can God truly use you? It's a fair question. But it's still just an excuse.

Fanny Crosby had age against her. Maybe you've never heard of old Fanny, but you've surely heard a few of her greatest hits; she was a hymnist and wrote such classic church ditties as "Blessed Assurance" and "To God Be the Glory." She wrote over 8,000 hymns and gospels. 8,000. Let that sink in.

That's a lot, right? Now consider the fact that she didn't write her first one until she was over forty. Now consider the fact that she was blind. She also wrote over 1,000 poems, and spoke before Congress to lobby for providing education to the blind.

It's never too late to become unstoppable. Fanny was blind. She was over forty. She had the perfect excuse. Nobody would have blamed her if she stayed home. But she let God use her disability to his glory. She proved what God proves time and time again: he uses the weak to show his strength. He takes everything you're bad at—every reason you have to say, "not me, God"—he takes it and he shows his glory. He shows the unexpected. When someone does something in the name of God that is expected, few people give another look; but when someone does the unexpected in God's name, people tend to give more than a nod their way.

APPENDIX

....

THE LEGACY OF THE DISCIPLES

istorically every disciple but John was martyred. There's a chance that two or three other disciples might have also died naturally. But how they died really doesn't matter; what matters, of course, is how they lived.

It's easy to say the disciples were unstoppable Christians, but to really understand how they developed before and after the Ascension, let's take a closer look at each disciple.

Andrew

Andrew wasn't one of the big three of the disciples, but he was certainly one of the key members of the all-star team. Like all the disciples, there are a lot of puzzle pieces that we can put together and begin to see who the disciple "probably" was. We know that Andrew was most likely Peter's brother. In most accounts, he is largely overshadowed by his brother, but his presence is still known and he was no doubt a key member of the early church. The Gospel of John notes that Andrew was a follower of John the Baptist and believed Jesus was the Messiah before his brother.[59]

The fact that Andrew, not Peter, is referenced as a follower of John the Baptist, tells us that he was probably the thinker of the family—while his brother was a hard worker, he was philosophical; it's no wonder that the apostle John, who was of the same temperament, remembers him more fondly than the other gospel accounts.[60]

In the New Testament, Andrew is best known for introducing people to Jesus. In John 1:41, Andrew, upon meeting Jesus, goes to Peter so he can introduce him. In John 6:9, Andrew introduces Jesus to a child who has five barley loaves and two fish. In John 12:20-22, two Greeks wanted an introduction to Jesus; they go to Philip who in turn goes to Andrew, who in turn goes with Philip to Jesus.

By these three accounts, we know something very important about who Andrew was: he found important people and brought them to Christ. He finds Peter who is obviously the Rock that Jesus built his church on; he finds the small child with the loaves who was a key component in the miracle—through him Jesus fed thousands. And he finds the Greeks; these were unclean people; a normal Jew would not

---

[59] John 1:41

[60] John and Andrew probably shared the same passions when it came to studying and reflecting on God's word.

have brought them to their teacher—their teacher would want nothing to do with them; but Andrew was able to understand—perhaps earlier than the other apostles—that Jesus was blind to races and skin colors—that these unclean people were key to his ministry and would be key to their own ministry.

There are lots of traditions about where Andrew went after the Ascension. We can assume he was very active in his missions work and started several churches.

More important than where he went was who he was. He was second string...but he was okay with that. While his brother was making a name for himself at the top of the pyramid, he was content in telling and bringing people to Christ. Through him, God shows us how he uses instruments—how our legacy is really in the people we bring to Christ—the role we played in the bigger picture. Without Andrew, then Peter would have never come to Christ. Think of all the most influential spiritual leaders in the world—someone introduced them to Christ; but those someones are rarely mentioned and when they are, people don't know who they are. That was Andrew.

It is almost universally accepted that Andrew was martyred. Legends have formed about how and where. The most popular is that he was crucified, but refused to be crucified as Christ was, and requested instead an X-shaped cross, which is now known as St. Andrew's Cross. Many country flags bear the symbol—notably Scotland, where Andrew is the Patron Saint.[61]

Bartholomew (Also Known as Nathanael)

Bartholomew was reluctant, to say the least, about Jesus; when Philip ran to him and told him that they had found the one Moses spoke of, he replied: Can anything good come from there (i.e. Nazareth)?[62] Jews in general didn't hold Nazareth in high regard—it was in Galilee, which Matthew 4:15 calls: "Galilee of the Gentiles." This was not the town for good Jewish boys and girls.

Philip didn't argue with Bartholomew and try and explain how indeed something good could come from Nazareth; he told Bartholomew to come and see for himself. And it doesn't take long to completely turn him around. When he meets Jesus, he almost instantly says, "Rabbi you are the Son of God; you are the king of Israel." (John 1:49)

Some of the disciples took a bit longer to recognize who Jesus was. Not Bartholomew. He went out of the gates run-

---

[61] This after a famous battle when the Scots were outnumbered and the King prayed that if they came out victorious he would name Andrew as the Patron Saint; it is said that an X appeared in the sky on the morning of battle.

[62] John 1:46

ning! Readers don't see a lot more about Bartholomew, but this verse alone tells us he was on fire for Jesus—it's hard to imagine that flame ever extinguished.

The tradition is that Bartholomew was a missionary in India and Armenia. A church was erected on the site that he is believed to have been martyred. How he was martyred is much speculated—theories range from beheaded to skinned alive. The reason for his martyrdom: converting the king of Armenia to Christianity.

James the Elder

James was one of the Brothers of Thunder—named, most likely, for their fiery spirit. He was the brother of the Apostle John—likely his older brother. Some believe that they were Jesus' cousins.

His father owned a successful fishing company and seems to have been a man making a very healthy living. His mom was Salome, who liked to pal around with the Marys and could easily be called an unofficial disciple.

James doesn't play a pivotal role in the gospels, but is a part of the close inner circle of apostles.

Acts 12:2 tells us that James was martyred; this was around 44 AD—approximately ten years after Christ ascended. James was both the first and only apostle that the Bible mentions was martyred. There is no record of why he was martyred—just who did it.[63] Many believe that James had gone to Spain to minister to Jews who had been exiled there, which did not go over well with Herod, who was the guy who sent them there.

After James, it really was game-on for the church. Up until this moment, they had perhaps been harassed and bullied—but this was an apostle—this was not supposed to happen to the leader of the church. Stephen had, of course, been the first martyr of the church, but his death was likely not as rippling as James'.

Christ had warned Christians that he did not come to bring peace, but the sword;[64] this was not a call to arms, rather a warning that they were now in a time of persecution. That warning was now real, and they had a choice to make: were they willing to die for the cross? James was the first, but not the last, to say yes.

James the Lesser or Younger

James the Lesser seems like an appropriate title because there's hardly anything known about him. Most hold he is the same as James, son of Alphaeus. Some hold that he is

---

[63] Herod Agrippa, whose granddad was responsible for murdering babies in Bethlehem.

[64] Matthew 10:34

the same as James, Brother of Jesus—but this is more debatable. The gospels typically list disciples in order of prominence—three groups: group one is the well-known ones, group two is the ones people know of, and group three are the most obscure ones. That's not to say they weren't important—or that people held them in lesser regard.

We can assume that James was not a leader—he was a follower; he didn't talk back—he listened.

James no doubt played a pivotal role in the growth of Christianity—he just wasn't as vocal as others. Perhaps he played more of a servant role than a leader role?

If you take the position that James the Lesser and James, Brother of Jesus were one in the same, then James became bishop of Jerusalem and was later martyred.

John

John was one of the few apostles who escaped martyrdom—perhaps the only apostle. Most believe John was the youngest apostle. Peter may have been the rock on which Christ built his church, but John was the one who lived to tell the church's story—dying when he was about 92.

It is traditionally accepted that John is the author of the Gospel of John, The Book of Revelations, and the First Epistle of John (many believe the other Epistles bearing his name were written by another John).

The stories he must have had to tell—he had seen all of his brothers and sisters in Christ die—suffering for what they believed. Unlike any other Christian in history, he was able to look back and see what had become of it—how it had grown and spread. Unlike the other gospels, which were written much earlier to convert believers, John's gospel seems to be an attempt to mature Christians—he's writing to make sure what really happened is documented. There were already people making up things about the church, and he wanted to make sure people knew the real story.

John was the philosopher of the group, and to him was tasked one of Christianity's greatest responsibilities: write the final book of the New Testament—the prophecy of what is to come.

It's likely that after his brother, James, suffered martyrdom, the apostles realized that they could no longer be close; if the church was to survive, then the disciples would have to scatter.

It is traditionally held that John wrote the Book of Revelations while in exile. According to this tradition, he was first put into boiling oil, but he did not die—he was not even burned.

Judas Iscariot

Judas committed suicide. Sunday school teaches us that much. So do pastors. Today we really don't think much about him. He's the guy who betrayed Jesus and killed himself.

But people thought differently thousands of years ago. While most certainly saw him as the betrayer, there are lots of stories about him.

The Gospel of Judas,[65] for example, tells an account of Jesus instructing Judas to betray him; Judas' action, therefore, was not an act of betrayal, rather of obedience. Judas, further, was given teachings the other disciples had not received.

If you believe in secret teachings, you might be a Gnostic, because that is essentially what's going on in the book. The book is dated, at the earliest, 120 AD, which means it came about much too late to being taken seriously as a canonical work—still, it shows us that *some* people did believed much differently about Judas than we do today.

In *The Gospel of Barnabas*,[66] Judas is transformed into the image of Jesus and takes his place at the crucifixion. How did Jesus rise from the dead? He didn't, according to this account, he never actually died—Judas did.

You can take the Sunday school version of Judas and say he's the guy responsible for Jesus' death, but if you believe that Jesus forgives all sins, then what about betrayal? In

---

[65] An Apocryphal work written in the second century.

[66] Dated even further than the Gospel of Judas—most give it a date in the 15th century at the earliest.

Matthew 26:50, Jesus calls Judas "friend" even when he knows what he's doing—he seems willing to forgive even in Judas' darkest moment. It should also be noted, however, that Judas never called Jesus Lord—he always referred to him as a Rabbi.

Was Judas forgiven? It certainly was a question on the mind of the early church. The answer really depends on whether he had finally concluded that Jesus was Lord. The Bible is clear that suicide is sin, but it's not the worst thing you can do—the worst thing is dying without realizing who Jesus really is.

Jude or Thaddeus

Just as Hitler pretty much killed the toothbrush mustache, Judas Iscariot sort of killed the name Judas; so much so that even the people in the Bible didn't want to include the name for fear people would associate it with *that* Judas. Case in point: that other apostle, Judas. Matthew and Mark call him Thaddeus; John calls him Judas not Iscariot; and Luke calls him Jude. Jude is what people know him as today.

Jude may or may not have written the Epistle of Jude; he also may or may not have been the brother of Jesus. He could have also been a cousin.

He may or may not have been vegetarians' best friend, because many traditions say he didn't eat meat. Jude the vegetarian stems from a work by Hegesippus,[67] who said that Jude did not drink alcohol or eat meat. Don't go running to your local library to dig up Hegesippus—his work is almost entirely lost, with the exception of a few quotes that Eusebius[68] uses.[69]

Jude is best known to Christians as the guy who asked a question. In John 14:22, he says during the Last Supper, "But, Lord, why do you intend to show yourself to us and not to the world?" (NIV)

According to tradition, Jude was martyred with Simon the Zealot.

Matthew or Levi

Matthew was originally a tax collector before Jesus called him to follow him. Traditionally, Matthew wrote the Gospel of Matthew, but the Gospel itself never makes reference to who the author is (or isn't) and the title "Gospel of

---

[67] A first century chronicler of Christianity.

[68] Another early church historian.

[69] And in case you're wondering, Jewish vegetarianism is actually a thing; it stems from the belief that the Torah implies Jews should maintain a meatless diet. And for the record, while the Torah does not directly forbid eating meat (except pork), it also does not say it's required.

Matthew" was not applied to it until years afterward. He may have written it; or he may not have.

There are elements of the Gospel that point to his authorship—the fact that it's written for a Jewish audience, for instance; also of note is the fact that three fifths of the Gospel is actual things that Jesus said—whoever wrote it had to have been there to record it.

Because of his status as a tax collector, we can assume that he had a significant amount of money, and before his call, all of the apostles either knew him or knew of him.

Traditionally, he died a martyr, but this has never been proven.

Peter or Simon Peter

Peter is the rock. The leader of the early Christian church—even the first Pope, if you are a Catholic. It is generally accepted that Peter wrote the first epistle of Peter, but the second is more debatable. Because the Gospel of Mark seems to have a Peter tone to it, it was originally thought to have been written by Peter's traveling companion, Mark; today, most scholars accept that there's no way to know who wrote the Gospel.

During Pentecost, it's Peter who gives the first sermon in all Christianity. Peter is fierier than ever, and it's clear who's going to lead the early movement of believers.

As passionate as Peter was to lead the church, he was slower to change it. He wasn't quite happy at first with how Gentiles should be treated; and he wasn't as far traveled as some of the other apostles. He's mostly seen managing the church.

Peter was martyred. Traditionally in Rome, but that most likely was not the case. Most believe it was ordered by Nero after the great fire of 64.[70] Some legends say upside down, but this is most likely not true.

Philip

There are two notable Philips in the Bible. Philip the Evangelist and Philip the Apostle. People often mistake the two as being the same person. Philip the Evangelist appears in the sixth and eighth chapter of the Acts of the Apostles— but he's not the same as the disciple.

If you always thought Philip the Apostle and Philip the Evangelist were one in the same, then you are not alone; many of the early church fathers felt the same way, which led to many apocryphal accounts that were simply false (Eusebius, one of the most noted early Christian fathers, was one of the people who got the two confused). How do we

---

[70] Nero blamed Christians for that fire—some say it was actually Nero who started the fire, but that is debatable.

know they aren't the same? The Bible tells us so. In Acts 6, the 12 disciples got together to pick seven deacons, and it lists this second Philip as one of the seven.

What do we know about Philip the Apostle? Not a lot.

We know that Philip isn't a Hebrew name, but he was Hebrew; that tells us that while his parents were Jewish, they were a little more liberal because they didn't pick a Jewish name.

John 1:44, tells us that he was from the city of Bethsaida, but John also notes that his was the town of Andrew and Peter—a note that has made some speculate that John is implying they were friends before Jesus. If that's the case, then Andrew, who, prior to becoming one of Jesus' disciples was a disciple of John the Baptist, probably had lots of long discussions with Philip about John's ministry.

Philip wasn't quick to come to a decision—in fact, Philip didn't find Jesus; Jesus found Philip. John 1:43 says, "The next day Jesus decided to leave for Galilee. Finding Philip, he said to him, 'Follow me.' (NIV) What's curious is Philip then goes to Nathanael in verse 45 and says, "We have found the one Moses wrote about in the law." (NIV) That seems like a mighty bold move on Philip's part since he didn't exactly find Jesus—but that's not what Philip is saying; he's not saying he went out seeking to find the Messiah and he did just that. He's saying he was empty, but he found the void to make him whole.

The fact that Philip is referencing Moses and the Old Testament tells us that he is a good Jewish boy who has no doubt heard about the coming Messiah; every Jew during this period was looking for the Messiah.

What else does the Bible tell us about Philip? It tells us more about his character—who he was as a person—than what he actually did.

John 6:1-15 shows Jesus preaching to a huge crowd—thousands of people; Jesus went to Philip and basically said, "Hey, we need to feed these people—they're hungry." Philip is puzzled—he has no idea how to do that, and tells Jesus it would take half a year's wage to buy enough bread for each person to have a single bite. It doesn't say what Jesus said to Philip—perhaps he didn't have time to say anything at all, because Andrew speaks up and tells Jesus about a boy with bread and fish.

John 12:21 shows two Gentiles asking Philip to get them an invitation to see Jesus; Philip in turn goes to Andrew, who goes with Philip to ask Jesus about it. That's not very exciting. Except it tells us two important things. First, it shows that Philip doesn't quite know what to do about Gentiles; and second, it shows his relationship with Andrew. Why can't Philip go alone to see Jesus about this Gentile question he has? The fact that John has mentioned Philip twice and both times Andrew is also mentioned tells us that the two were probably pretty close.

In John 14, we see Philip one final time; in the Upper Room before his crucifixion, Philip challenges Jesus; Jesus tells his disciples in 14:6-7 that he is "the way and the truth and the life. No one comes to the Father except through me. If you really know me, you will know my Father as well.

From now on, you do know him and you have seen him."
(NIV) He's telling his disciples that he is God! It's a divine
moment! And then Philip speaks up...

He tells Jesus in verse 8 that if he shows them the Father,
then that will be enough.

What Jesus says in reply to this is basically an epic, "Are
you kidding me, Philip?!" For the next several verses, Jesus
reiterates who the Father is.

Some of the disciples are bold. Some are rather quiet.
And some are simply ordinary. Philip was of the ordinary
variety. There really was nothing special about him. He
wasn't bold—and when he is bold, it's about something he
shouldn't be bold about. But God took this ordinary man
and he used him to his glory.

After the Ascension, non-Biblical tradition says that he
became a missionary in what is now the country of Turkey—not too far from Ephesus, where the Apostle John
eventually settled.

And again, going off tradition, Philip performed a miracle in what is now the country of Turkey on the wife of a
high-ranking city official; through the miracle and his teaching he converted her. This didn't go over well with her husband, who ordered Philip and Bartholomew to be crucified
upside-down. Bartholomew was eventually released, but
Philip supposedly asked that he himself be left on the cross.
Was he martyred? Probably. Was he martyred in this way?
Probably not. There were other traditions about what happened, but they conflict. There are enough traditions to make
it easy to speculate that he indeed was killed. It's just hard to

say how. In 2011, archaeologists uncovered a tomb that some believe belongs to Philip. The tomb is in Turkey in the region he is believed to have been martyred.

Simon the Zealot

Simon the Zealot is the most obscure of all the apostles. He was an apostle—that much the Bible tells us. But that's about all we know.

We also know he was a Zealot. A Zealot? Not familiar with the group? They were basically the Jewish mafia. You didn't want to mess around with them. The group started as a way of getting the Roman Empire out of the Holy Land. The Jews had been ridiculously taxed.[71] These weren't the Bernie Sanders kind of fanatics who waved their hands in the air and rallied people up but were ultimately peaceful; these were the stabby kind of fanatics—the kind that would stab anyone they thought to be a traitor.

So, Simon was a knife-carrying member of his local Zealot club? Possibly, but probably not. Not all Zealots were as radical as others. The main component of all Zealots was they wanted Rome out of their land.

---

[71] Some say up to 40% of their income went to taxes—and no, they weren't able to write off their lambs as a tax deduction.

When you look at all the disciples, you begin to see that they each had unique characteristics that made them a diverse—yet perfect—bunch. You had the leaders, the philosophers, and the caregivers. And you have Simon the Zealot—a man willing to carry his passions to the extreme. The Zealots were a violent bunch of revolutionaries; the disciples were peace-loving group of revolutionaries—the contrast here is hard to miss. One cannot say with certainty why Jesus picked the disciples he picked, but one cannot help but see how he turned a man who must have been full of fiery rage into a man who was full of fiery love.

There are lots of stories of what happened to Simon the Zealot—some say he traveled as far as England; most believe he was martyred—murdered, no doubt, by the souls full of the same rage he used to have.

Thomas

Thomas doubted. That's what the Bible tells us. That's what he's remembered for. And that's a shame because Thomas did so much more than doubt—realistically, that's the least he should be remembered for. But Thomas probably wouldn't mind much, because it was as a result of that doubt that he accomplished so much. He lived the rest of his days doubting no more.

Some believe that Thomas was the twin brother of Matthew; his name, Thomas, means twin, so it's easy to believe that he was the twin of someone. Some also believe that Matthew was the prodigal son in the parable that Jesus tells; if that's true, then Thomas was the brother who stayed home—who was cautious, which fits his personality.

Thomas is remembered by Catholics as being present at the assumption of Mary—a doctrine Protestants do not traditionally accept—where, according to legends, Thomas was in India when he was transported to her tomb to witness her assumption into Heaven.

It's widely accepted that Thomas was a missionary in India until his death; in fact, he traveled perhaps more than any other disciple.

Some of the earliest apocryphal writings have born Thomas' name;[72] while the writings are too late to be included in the Bible,[73] they do tell us how interested people were in the life of this doubter.

Most believe that Thomas died as a Martyr in India.

Matthias 12th Disciple After Judas Betrayed

---

[72] Including the Infancy Gospel of Thomas about the boyhood of Jesus; the Gospel of Thomas, which consist of sayings of Jesus; and the Acts of Thomas, which is largely about his missions after the Ascension.

[73] The dating is about 100 to 300 AD.

Matthias is an easy apostle to forget. He's mentioned in Acts 1:23-26 and then is essentially forgotten—but not gone. While the Bible is void of Matthias, he had a very active ministry.

We know that Matthias, while not an original disciple, was with Jesus during his ministry; it was one of the requirements for being chosen—he had to be an eyewitness of Jesus and see the Resurrection. This is what we know with absolute certainty. From here, we have to start leaning a lot on tradition.

Tradition tells us that he did a lot of church planting in what is now Turkey and Georgia. Again, according to tradition, he was stoned to death in Georgia. There is a marker for his grave in Georgia, but that does not necessarily mean that's where he's buried—there are lots of claims about where disciples were buried. There are also claims that he was stoned in Jerusalem as well as what is now Turkey.

About the only thing anyone seems to agree with is that he died a martyr.

UNSTOPPABLE CHRISTIANS

The disciples were sort of the all-star team. In 1885, there was another sort of all-star team making waves around the country: The Cambridge Seven.

The Cambridge Seven was composed of six Cambridge students and one from the Royal Military Academy. These were men who came from well-to-do families; men who knew that a life of comfort awaited them after college. But comfort didn't quite suit them.

At the time, Hudson Taylor was making waves of his own by opening up China to missionaries. Christianity had been in China prior to Taylor, and there were certainly other missionaries in China; but Taylor is most commonly cited for opening the floodgates. Through his mission,[74] over 800 missionaries came to the country and opened over 125 schools. Taylor didn't just come to the country as some missionaries did—he immersed himself in the country by wearing their clothes, learning their culture and speaking their language.

The Cambridge Seven heard Taylor and accepted his call to be missionaries in China.

They were paraded around England and used as examples of how God can turn anyone into a missionary. Men who believed God didn't want them to be comfortable...he wanted them to be unstoppable.

While not all seven stayed in China for their entire lives, all seven remained in ministry.

---

[74] China Inland Mission.

APPENDIX B

....

REFERENCE TO THE
ASCENSION

Psalm 47:5 - God has ascended amid shouts of joy, the LORD amid the sounding of trumpets. (NIV)
Psalm 68:18 - When you ascended on high, you took many captives; you received gifts from people, even from the rebellious—that you, LORD God, might dwell there. (NIV)
Mark 16:19 - After the Lord Jesus had spoken to them, he was taken up into heaven and he sat at the right hand of God. (NIV)
Luke 24:26 - Did not the Messiah have to suffer these things and then enter his glory? (NIV)
Luke 24:50-51 - When he had led them out to the vicinity of Bethany, he lifted up his hands and blessed them. 51 While he was blessing them, he left them and was taken up into heaven. (NIV)
John 1:51 - He then added, "Very truly I tell you, you will see 'heaven open, and the angels of God ascending and descending on' the Son of Man." (NIV)

John 6:62 - Then what if you see the Son of Man ascend to where he was before! (NIV)

John 7:33-34 - Jesus said, "I am with you for only a short time, and then I am going to the one who sent me. 34 You will look for me, but you will not find me; and where I am, you cannot come." (NIV)

John 7:39 - By this he meant the Spirit, whom those who believed in him were later to receive. Up to that time the Spirit had not been given, since Jesus had not yet been glorified. (NIV)

John 14:2-4 - My Father's house has many rooms; if that were not so, would I have told you that I am going there to prepare a place for you? 3 And if I go and prepare a place for you, I will come back and take you to be with me that you also may be where I am. 4 You know the way to the place where I am going." (NIV)

John 14:12 - Very truly I tell you, whoever believes in me will do the works I have been doing, and they will do even greater things than these, because I am going to the Father. (NIV)

John 14:28 - "You heard me say, 'I am going away and I am coming back to you.' If you loved me, you would be glad that I am going to the Father, for the Father is greater than I. (NIV)

John 16:5 - but now I am going to him who sent me. None of you asks me, 'Where are you going?' (NIV)

John 16:7 - But very truly I tell you, it is for your good that I am going away. Unless I go away, the Advocate will not come to you; but if I go, I will send him to you. (NIV)

John 16:10 - about righteousness, because I am going to the Father, where you can see me no longer; (NIV)

John 16:16 - Jesus went on to say, "In a little while you will see me no more, and then after a little while you will see me." (NIV)

John 16:25 - "Though I have been speaking figuratively, a time is coming when I will no longer use this kind of language but will tell you plainly about my Father. (NIV)

John 16:28 - I came from the Father and entered the world; now I am leaving the world and going back to the Father." (NIV)

John 17:5 - And now, Father, glorify me in your presence with the glory I had with you before the world began. (NIV)

John 17:13 - "I am coming to you now, but I say these things while I am still in the world, so that they may have the full measure of my joy within them. (NIV)

John 20:17 - Jesus said, "Do not hold on to me, for I have not yet ascended to the Father. Go instead to my brothers and tell them, 'I am ascending to my Father and your Father, to my God and your God.'" (NIV)

Acts 1:9 - After he said this, he was taken up before their very eyes, and a cloud hid him from their sight. (NIV)

Acts 3:21 - Heaven must receive him until the time comes for God to restore everything, as he promised long ago through his holy prophets. (NIV)

Romans 8:34 - Who then is the one who condemns? No one. Christ Jesus who died—more than that, who was raised to life—is at the right hand of God and is also interceding for us. (NIV)

Ephesians 1:20 - he exerted when he raised Christ from the dead and seated him at his right hand in the heavenly realms, (NIV)

Ephesians 4:8-10 - This is why it says: "When he ascended on high, he took many captives and gave gifts to his people." 9 (What does "he ascended" mean except that he also descended to the lower, earthly regions? 10 He who descended is the very one who ascended higher than all the heavens, in order to fill the whole universe.) (NIV)

Philippians 2:9-11 - Therefore God exalted him to the highest place and gave him the name that is above every name, 10 that at the name of Jesus every knee should bow, in heaven and on earth and under the earth, 11 and every tongue acknowledge that Jesus Christ is Lord, to the glory of God the Father. (NIV)

1 Timothy 3:16 Beyond all question, the mystery from which true godliness springs is great: He appeared in the flesh, was vindicated by the Spirit, was seen by angels, was preached among the nations, was believed on in the world, was taken up in glory. (NIV)

Hebrews 1:3 - The Son is the radiance of God's glory and the exact representation of his being, sustaining all things by his powerful word. After he had provided purification for sins, he sat down at the right hand of the Majesty in heaven. (NIV)

Hebrews 4:14 - Therefore, since we have a great high priest who has ascended into heaven, Jesus the Son of God, let us hold firmly to the faith we profess. (NIV)

Jesus Ascended. What Does That Mean?

Hebrews 9:24 - For Christ did not enter a sanctuary made with human hands that was only a copy of the true one; he entered heaven itself, now to appear for us in God's presence. (NIV)

1 Peter 3:22 - who has gone into heaven and is at God's right hand—with angels, authorities and powers in submission to him. (NIV)

....

TIMELINE OF EVENTS

- Jesus appears to Mary Magdalene (Mark 16:9-11, John 20:11-18)
- Jesus appears to Mary, Salome, Joanna (Matthew 28:1, Mark 16:1, Luke 24:10)
- Jesus appears to Peter (Luke 24:34)
- Jesus appears to Cleopas and his companion (Luke 24:13-35)
- Jesus appears to the disciples (minus Thomas) (Luke 24:36-43, John 20:19-25)
- Jesus appears to disciples (including Thomas) (John 20:26-29)
- Seven of the disciples at the Sea of Tiberius (John 21:1-23)
- Disciples and a large gathering at Galilee (Matthew 28:16-17)
- The Ascension (Luke 24:50-52)
- Pentecost (Acts 2:1-40)

....

DISCUSSION QUESTIONS

Prologue

1. What was Easter like for you as a child? Share a few memories.
2. Have you ever thought about the Ascension? What does it mean to you?
3. Do you think the Ascension is essential to Christian faith? If it didn't happen, would it matter?
4. Each Gospel has a different message and audience. Which one speaks to you the most and why?
5. Have you ever met a Christian who seems to have unstoppable faith? What stands out about them?

Chapter 1

1. Can you remember the first time you heard the Resurrection story? If not, share when the story became more significant for you?
2. When Jesus rises, nobody actually sees it; he just starts appearing to people. It's very subtle. Why do you think this is?
3. Why do you think Jesus appeared to the women before anyone else?
4. Do you think it's unusual that the women do not recognize Jesus? Do you think he looked different, or do you think the women are just in shock?
5. If Jesus appeared to you, what's the first thing you would do? Who would you tell? Would it change the way you believe, or make you more devoted?

Chapter 2

1. Have you ever had a mysterious encounter or a time where you felt a divine intervention?
2. Jesus gave a Bible study to the two men; if Jesus walked into your Bible study and could give a lesson on any book or topic in the Bible, what would you want it to be?
3. Jesus scolded these men for their weak belief; do you think Jesus would scold you?
4. Why do you think these men were "kept" from recognizing Jesus?
5. What does it mean to walk by faith not by sight?

Chapter 3

1. There's a meeting with Peter that is never explained in the Bible—except to say it happened—what do you think happened?
2. When the women tell the disciples about what happened, Peter and John take off running. If someone told you that Jesus had appeared at a specific location, how would you approach it? Would you run? Walk? Wait and see what others think? See if Fox News covers the story?
3. Why do you think the disciples are so afraid when Jesus returns?
4. The disciples think Jesus is a ghost at first; why can't Jesus be a ghost? Do you think ghosts are real? If so, what role do you think they play?
5. What does it mean to "receive the Holy Spirit"?

Chapter 4

1. Share a time when you felt you missed out on something.
2. Put yourself in Thomas' shoes; all your friends have seen Jesus and you have not. How would you feel? Would you believe your friends? Or would you be skeptical?

3. If you go to church, do you feel comfortable or challenged? If you don't go to church, what keeps you away?
4. The Bible doesn't say what happened after Thomas believed. What do you think happened? Do you think Jesus simply left? Do you think there was a teaching?
5. Do you believe stigmata is a real thing?

Chapter 5

1. Is there a place you like to escape to? A home away from home?
2. Do you think it's odd that after Jesus appeared to the disciples, they go back to work? Would life go on as usual for you?
3. Picture yourself in the boat with the disciples; Jesus appears on the shore. Who would you be? Would you be like Peter jumping into the water so you can get there quicker? Would you stay in the boat? Would you row the other way because you're terrified of what Jesus would say to you?
4. Why do you think Jesus let them catch so many fish—especially when he'd already prepared a meal for them?
5. What do you think is the significance of Jesus asking Peter three times if he loves him?

Chapter 6

1. Have you ever gone on a mission trip? If so, share where you went and what the trip meant to you. Did you grow at all? If you haven't, is there anything that holds you back or is it something you would like to do one day?

2. Jesus has now appeared to all of them and yet during the Great Commission, it says that some of them still doubted. How is that even possible? What do you think their thought process is?

3. Jesus rebukes them for doubting; we often hear about the loving side of Jesus, but not so much the rebuking side—does it surprise you when you hear about this side of Jesus? Is there anything in your life that you think he'd be disappointed by?

4. What does baptism mean to you? When were you baptized and what did it mean to you? If you haven't been baptized, is there anything that holds you back from it?

5. Is there anyone or any group that you feel called to share the Gospel with, but you are afraid to?

Chapter 7

1. Have you ever heard a really weird non-Biblical story about Jesus?

2. Even if apocryphal works aren't true, do you think we should study them?

3. Does anything surprise you about the apocryphal works the author mentions?

4. Do you think Mary was a virgin for life? Do you think this is an important teaching? Why or why not?

5. Do you think Jesus appearing to 500 and 120 is the same thing? If not, what do you think happened when he appeared to 500, and why isn't it recorded in more detail?

Chapter 8

1. If you knew you were going to die, what would your last words be?

2. What do you think the Ascension looked like?

3. Do you think the Ascension was something that spiritually happened or physically happened?

4. What does it mean to you when it says in Ephesians 4:8 that Christ led "captivity captive"?

5. What does worship mean to you?

Chapter 9

1. What's something in your life that you feel you were unprepared for—that you were just kind of tossed into? How did you get through it?

2. Why do you think Jesus Ascended after forty days? Why not 3? Why not 300? What's so special about forty?

3. Why is Pentecost so important? And why is there not the same emphasis placed on it as Easter or Christmas?

4. What does it mean to you to be filled with the Holy Spirit?

5. Do you think people can still speak in tongues today? Why or why not?

Chapter 10

1. What disciple do you relate to?

2. Did any of the post-Resurrection lives of the disciples jump out at you or surprise you?

3. If you were a disciple, do you think you would be in Jesus' inner circle?

4. Do you think you could die for your faith? If so, do you think it makes you weak in faith if you can't die for it or are afraid to die for it?

5. Do you think Judas was forgiven?

Epilogue

1. Would Christianity change for you if Christ had simply risen from the dead, lived out his days, and died of natural causes?
2. What does it mean to be members of Christ's body?
3. What does Christ's command to make disciples mean to you?
4. What spiritual gifts do you have?
5. What would you look like as an unstoppable Christian?

ABOUT THE AUTHOR

Scott Douglas wrote this about page, which, he admits, makes him sound a bit like a narcissist; so narcissistically speaking, Douglas is the esteemed author of a memoir about his experience working in a public library (*Quiet, Please: Dispatches from a Public Librarian*), an ongoing YA series (*The N00b Warriors*), and two technical books on iPhone app development (*Going Mobile* and *Build Your Own Apps for Fun and Profit*). Esteemed writing aside, Douglas teaches humor and memoir writing for the Gotham Writers Workshops. He lives in Anaheim, but to sound cooler, he usually says he "lives five minutes from Disneyland." He lives with his wife, Diana, in a home that is a registered California landmark. His burps smell like roses.

If Scott Douglas did not write this about page, it would read:
Scott Douglas lives in Anaheim with his wife. He is the author of other books. He likes to think that his organic deodorant holds back his BO for more than 30 minutes, but who is he kidding?

CPSIA information can be obtained
at www.ICGtesting.com
Printed in the USA
FFHW020641020120
57418718-62877FF